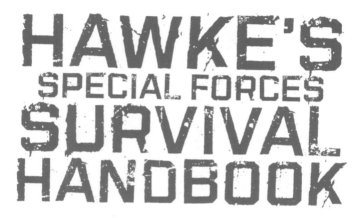

HAWKE'S SPECIAL FORCES SURVIVAL HANDBOOK

The Portable Guide to Getting Out Alive

BY MYKEL HAWKE

Captain in the U.S. Army Special
Forces and Director of Spec Ops Inc.

RUNNING PRESS
PHILADELPHIA • LONDON

9 8 7 6 5
Digit on the right indicates the number of this printing

Library of Congress Control Number: 2010937313
ISBN 978-0-7624-4064-1

Cover and interior design by Matthew Goodman
Edited by Greg Jones
Interior illustrations by Dale Hodgkinson
Typography: Caslon and Myriad

Running Press Book Publishers
2300 Chestnut Street
Philadelphia, PA 19103-4371

Visit us on the web!
www.runningpress.com
www.mykelhawke.com

CONTENTS

Chapter 1:
**THE PSYCHOLOGY
OF SURVIVAL . . . 4**

Chapter 2:
SHELTER . . . 18

Chapter 3:
WATER . . . 39

Chapter 4:
FIRE . . . 70

Chapter 5:
FOOD . . . 102

Chapter 6:
TOOLS . . . 142

Chapter 7:
NAVIGATION . . . 154

Chapter 8:
SIGNALS . . . 184

Chapter 9:
FIRST AID . . . 191

Chapter 10:
NATURE . . . 251

1

THE
PSYCHOLOGY
OF SURVIVAL

It happens to thousands of people every year, and it could just as easily happen to you. Your airplane goes down in the wilderness; or the train you're riding derails miles from the nearest junction; or your car breaks down in the desert; or you get lost while hiking in the woods; or a snowstorm strands you in the mountains unprepared . . . the possibilities are endless.

In any case, you may survive the initial trauma event only to quickly realize that you are now in a terrible, dangerous predicament. It's possible that everyone who was with you has died, including your spouse, child, or friend; or maybe some have also survived. It's likely that you or others have sustained bad injuries. You may find that you have little-to-no resources available—no food or water, no tools, no communication device, and no clue where you are or how to get to someplace safe. But the biggest question of all is whether or not you will be able to handle the reality of the situation in your head and heart: **Do you have the will to survive?**

This book is for anyone who would hope to be prepared should they find themselves in such dire straits. The general survival situation I talk about inside this book is the kind that no one chooses to place themselves into—in other words, this is not for hikers or mountaineers or skilled outdoorsmen. And the information and skills I provide are meant to be grasped and applied by anyone. By far the most important factor in anyone's survival in these cases is not only the topic of this first chapter, but it is something that anyone can develop and carry with them at all times. That is, a strong psychology for survival—the will to live.

You must say this right now—"I will do everything and anything it takes to stay alive and to keep going with every ounce of my physical and spiritual energy, until I get back home and into the hearts of the ones I love."

I am telling you right now that this is the single most important lesson in this book: Never quit!

Preparation at Fort Living Room

The general rules of life clearly state that if you're ready for something, it won't happen; and if you ain't ready, it sure will happen! This phenomenon is sometimes called "Murphy's Law" (or "Sod's Law" in the UK) and I have found that it also translates perfectly into "Hawke's Law of Survival." So when I travel, I always have a little chuckle to myself thinking, "If this plane goes down and anyone survives, it probably won't be me, but rather someone who wouldn't even know how to use half my travel survival kit, providing they even thought to look for it, haha!" I'll be the dead guy with all the handy stuff on his body, so search me well if you happen to be on my flight!

Okay, this gives you a feel for my sense of humor. You'll see that I apply it throughout the book, and heck, throughout my life for that matter. You'd be surprised at how a sense of humor can benefit you in the worst of situations. Look at it like this: it'd be pretty funny to survive a plane crash or boat sinking, and then die from lack of food or water! But look at the upside—either way, if you die fast, there's no suffering; if you die of starvation or exposure, well, at least you had time to make peace with your maker. You see, either way and in all things, I suggest you always look for the positive, and don't dwell on the negative any more than you need to in order to identify it and learn not to repeat whatever caused it. If something you're doing or thinking ain't fixing or improving your situation, it's wasting your time. And the clock is always ticking towards your death, so don't squander one moment in unproductive depression or self-pity or any of the other things that only serve to drain your energy without benefit.

Now, don't get me wrong: of course you should take some time—after you've done all you can to handle the immediate disaster and are having a well-deserved and well-timed break—to give things a think, even have a cry. This is healthy if controlled, and even necessary for your psyche. We must mourn if we experienced loss, and usually with a survival situation, there is loss. And accept the possibility that more anguish may be on the way—otherwise, you will fear it, and fear will beat you down faster than anything and spread like a virus. It will consume you in a heartbeat and even spread to others very quickly if you're in a group.

That is why combat commanders cannot tolerate fear in the ranks. Fear is *that* dangerous, and you should view **fear** as your worst enemy in any survival situation. The way we as commanders manage it, is to keep the troops busy and productive. All that apparent "busywork" that soldiers always seem to be doing has a purpose—commanders are making sure the men don't have time for fear to set in. You should do the same.

You see, most fear is a result of ignorance; it's a fear of the unknown. By sitting down in Fort Living Room, right now, learning techniques and gaining confidence in your knowledge of what to do, you are putting yourself in a better position to handle a survival situation when you're in a real hurt box.

Now, reading and thinking about it is better than nothing, but nothing is better than hands-on experience when it comes to the survival arts. So **get prepared** by reading this book, trying many of the skills and techniques within, getting good at the ones that feel most natural to you, and practicing them every once in a while. This will give you the hard skills and confidence that will keep you prepared for anything. And that is the number-one way to fight fear—to know what to do.

No matter whether you are a man, woman, child, old, young, fit, or even disabled—I don't give a rat's butt, frankly—you can make it as long as you work on your basics, know what you want to live for, and never quit. Heart, Mind, and Skills (in that order!) vanquish fear. This is the key to survival.

The most important skill you can have and develop is

simply good old-fashioned common sense. And before we get into what it takes to be prepared, let's talk for a moment about *not* being prepared. As in Murphy's Law of combat, you'll likely find yourself in a survival situation right on the day you decide to go to the store to buy a bunch of survival stuff!

Ultimately you need to be mentally prepared for the harsh realties of surviving. Death is real and a real possibility always. The key is, if you find yourself in a bad situation and you have nothing: **Then** you are surviving!

When you have nothing, this commitment is all you have, and, more times than not, this can actually be enough. You don't stop to think and let the fear get a grip, you just keep driving on and never quit. Keeping a grip on one's courage has carried countless many through almost certain in battle, and so it can serve you, too, in the battle for survival. I cannot repeat or stress enough the mantra: **Never quit!**

Of course the survival situation is quite a different reality than that of the combat soldier. However, the potential end result is the same. Dead is dead. And it is in this way that the psychology of survival is applicable both to soldiers and survivors.

Tools & Toys

Obviously, most survival scenarios happen instantly and without warning, so it's unlikely that you will have any tools at all on your person to help you through. Or is it?

I always carry at least a minimal "survival kit" most places I go. I'll discuss these in detail in Chapter 10. But for now, let's look at some of the most practical survival tools—or "toys" as we sometimes call 'em—you should consider carrying whenever you travel.

Communications

First and foremost is communications. Let's face it, the best way outta trouble is the most direct and easiest—pick up the bat phone and call for the rescue limo service.

Satellite phones, cell phones, radios, and other signaling devices like laser lights, strobes, beacons, transponders, flares, etc. are all available. Get them, keep them.

I always look for size and weight first. The reason is simple: if it's too big and bulky, it becomes cumbersome and eventually gets left behind. Murphy's Law of Combat states: "The day you leave it behind, even after years of carrying it without use, will be the very day you need it most." So, carry everything all the time and always test these devices.

Knives, Tools, and Other Gizmos

Everything you can get, and carry, is good. And anything is always better than nothing. But make it count. Check it out before you're down and out—remember: keep it light!

As for knives and tools, for every pro there is a con. A big knife is great for whacking down trees to make a shelter, a raft, a sled, etc. But, they not only make it really hard to do small stuff like make snares and traps, they can actually be dangerous.

The same goes for knives that are too small. These are great for most jobs around the camp for surviving, but they sure make it hard to build a shelter. Try for a middle ground.

The number-one tool in survival is the knife. Always carry one or have one available and/or accessible. And learn a few ways to make or improvise different knives.

One of Murphy's/Sod's Laws is that there are no Atheists in foxholes. That means, when you're in battle and bullets are flying, folks who do not believe in God or some spiritual entity by any name, tend to find themselves making prayers to someone or something when it looks like death is an imminent potentiality. And the same holds true for those surviving: all of a sudden, you figure out what matters to you most and what you believe in, if you hadn't before.

Murphy's Laws of Combat and Hawke's Laws of Survival

Let me share with you a few of Murphy's Laws of Combat, as they're extremely relevant to Hawke's Laws of Survival. For you vets, these will remind you of the tickle you got the first time you learned them in practice. For those of you not familiar with them, they will give you a great insight into the realities of survival, since survival really is combat between you and nature, a fight to live. And nature is always stronger, you never defeat her, you only overcome her challenges. Respecting the laws of combat is tantamount to respecting the laws of nature. You will be better off for it in both instances.

Murphy's Laws of Combat (just a few, as there are many)
If it's stupid but it works, it ain't stupid
No plan ever survives first contact with the enemy
The enemy attacks on two occasions—when he's ready, and, when you're not
No inspection-ready unit ever passed in combat, and no combat-ready unit ever passed inspection
When you are short everything but enemy, you're in combat
When the battle is going your way, you're in an ambush or trap

Hawke's Laws of Survival (for starters. . . .)
Never quit
Everything you plan and pack, will be lost in the event that causes the survival scenario
Survival situations happen to those who haven't studied, or have but aren't ready
The best-trained, most-equipped survivalist will be the first one killed in the crash
The person least likely to survive will be the one left to face surviving
When you lack everything but misery, you are surviving
When you think you got it all handled, you're in the biggest trouble

Ecological Footprint

When I encounter people who don't want to chop a small tree for their shelter in the cold, or they don't want to kill a small mammal for their meal, then I hand them a pencil and paper. I ask them, "Who is the most important person alive on this planet that you love and care for?" Then I tell them to write this letter:

"Dear Jonnie/Janie,
    I love you very much, but I love this tree or this critter more than you, so, I refuse to kill it. Therefore, I will lay down here and die. But know that I love you, very much, just not as much as this rabbit or bush."
    They always chop or kill after that. . . .

Should I Stay or Should I Go

The second key decision you will have to make after a tragic event leaves you in a survival situation is: Should I stay or should I go? (The first, of course, is: "Do I want to live, or am I gonna give up right now because it's all just too much." By now, you know the answer to that question. **Hint: Never Quit!**)

Before you can start considering food, water, fire, shelter, and other necessities, you must first assess your immediate circumstances. If your life is in peril, you must remedy that condition. If someone else is in peril, too, and you assess that you can get them and yourself out at the same time, then do not hesitate to snatch them up and scoot. However, if you got a snapped arm, and they've got double broken legs, then it's not heroism but rather foolishness to try and pull them and you out, if the plane is about to go over a cliff, for example. In the first moments, it's all about heartbeat assessments and split-second decisions. Many folks can and will second-guess themselves later, but that is for then, not now. If you're a fitness stud and conditions are right, go for the heroism. If you're hungover, or sick, or otherwise weak, and you just know you can't get them too, then get yourself out—otherwise, there is just one more dead person and that would be a tragic waste as you might have saved ten people later if you had lived. Now if your child or lover is in danger, and you'd rather not live without them, no rules, go for it—do all you can to save them regardless of your position or the situation. Either way, your problems will be solved.

But once you have yourself and others out of immediate harm's way, and you've treated yourself and others—as **first aid** is the real first priority of survival—then you make the decision to **stay** where you are and wait for help, or **go**, evacuating the immediate area and looking for ways out. Stay Or Go = (the SOG-y plan)

This decision will determine everything that follows. What to bring, what to leave, what to use now, what to ration; these are all answered based on this one key decision—to stay or to go.

Now sometimes you won't even have an option. If your ship sinks, you're pretty much stranded right where it sunk unless you have a lifeboat. But without it, you're stuck at the mercy of the seas, currents, winds, and other elements at play. In these cases, you just start working on improving your situation, seeking refuse, debris, other survivors, etc.

But when it is an option to stay or go, the general thinking is most of the time it is better to stay put. Especially nowadays when most aircraft, sea vessels, and other forms of transport are tied into radio, satellite, and navigation systems that tell others back in civilization where that transport is and where it isn't, when it should have reported in, and when it didn't make its last required communications.

For these reasons, most of the time, the right answer is to stay put. Even when you are alone in a broken down vehicle or at a campsite, these things have a larger footprint than a lone individual walking around by themselves. This means it will be easier for someone to find you if you are lost or stranded. Staying put near a crash site will highly increase the chances of being found and ultimately surviving.

In these cases, figure out what the priorities are. In most cases, water will be the very first priority, but, if you're in a harsh environment, shelter might be the top priority. And if very cold or wet, fire might be more immediately important than water. But in all cases, make water a priority and when not number one, keep in mind that it is always a close number two unless you happen to have plenty of it on hand.

Of course, there will be situations in which you will come to realize that your best chances of survival will be to pack up and start walking. In some cases, the place you're at will be so inhospitable that extended survival there doesn't seem likely. In other cases, you may do all you can to survive for several days or even weeks at the scene of the disaster while hoping that rescuers are on the way, and then finally decide that no one is coming to save you, in which case you would have to seriously consider making a plan and heading out to find your own rescue.

Whether you stay or go, the priorities of survival remain the same. The constants are: **shelter, water, food, and fire**. Their order is variable, but these factors are not. Remember the acronym: S.W.F.F. In other words, you need to think and act "SWiFFly" in all things survival.

We'll discuss these things in detail in each specific chapter. For now, it is enough to know that you must make a decision early on to stay or to go. The rest of your dramatic story will unfold and be told as you go from that fork in the road.

Make a Plan and Plan on Changes!

Always make a plan, no matter what. It gives you (and others, if present) a starting point. It helps you to keep focused and on-track when things happen to confuse or interrupt your efforts.

But remember Murphy's Law: No plan survives first contact with the enemy. The same is true for you in a survival situation. Rarely will anything you plan work out just the way you think or envision. In fact, it is best to plan on having numerous changes in the plan!

And when it comes to initial decisions and moves, remember the acronym "D.A.P.R. S.O.G." In other words, "DAPpeR before SOGgy." This relates to four elements:

- **Danger:** Get out of harm's way, and get others out of harm's way if you safely can.
- **Assistance:** Provide first aid to yourself and others.
- **Prioritize:** Assess the situation and prioritize the SWFF constants (shelter, water, fire, food).
- **Reality:** Decide to stay or go.

Ration and plan for the long haul, no matter what your circumstances and decisions, as it is the case more times than not that folks are stranded far longer than they ever anticipate. Whether you opt to stay at the site or make a move, rationing is the smart move.

Ancient Chinese Wisdom: Expectation Is the Source of All Unhappiness

One of the fundamental keys to your survival is to not expect anything.

Do not expect to be rescued; you will only be let down, disheartened, and disillusioned if it doesn't come to pass. Do not expect to have any creature comforts; you will only become angry, frustrated, and fatigued when you don't have them. Do not expect that anything will go right or go your way or be easy; you will only lose interest, drive, and motivation at every corner when they don't.

Expect nothing. Expect no one to do anything for you. Expect no one to find you. Expect not to live. This is your reality. You must accept this and live in this very moment this way. To expect to get out and walk away is to fear the opposite if it happens. To fear is to freeze, and to freeze can be the very thing that causes what you fear to happen.

The point of this Asian concept is to live right here, right now, in this present moment.

Expectation is different than hope. Hope for everything. Believe in yourself. Dream of your return to better times, see it and envision a happy ending. Do this in the slow moments, or the quiet, cold, wet, or hot moments when you can do nothing else but think. But then, when that time has passed and it's time to work or move, put those thoughts away and hold no expectations of their fruition. Keep all of these alive and within you, and nurture them every day and re-kindle them when doused, so as to never let them fade and pass. **But do not expect**.

As the ancient Chinese wisdom says, expectation is the source of all unhappiness. It is true. It is a false seed that will not bear fruit. Do not plant it; do not let it take root. Rip it out if it does begin to grow in you, and do this with a vengeance.

Expect nothing. Hope for everything.

Remember: Choose Life; Kill to Live; be DAPpeR before SOGgy; think SWiFFly; and above all, **Never quit!**

This is all I have to say on Survival Psychology.

2

SHELTER

Easiest first is the rule for shelters.

Look around you and make what you have work for you. If you have a broken down vehicle, aircraft, sea vessel, or any wreckage or building debris, use it.

Be aware that building a shelter takes time, and a good one takes work and therefore energy—especially to make it windproof and waterproof. If you are lucky enough to have all that sorted out for you, or if you're in such a pleasant climate that you can do without, then maybe consider not even making a shelter. Forget that! In the best of conditions, I still recommend using something for cover. Weather can change quickly, night temperatures may be very different than daytime temperatures, and most of all, you never know what critters and creepy crawlers are about. Just don't risk it.

So, first use what you have. If you don't have a ready-made shelter, use what is readily available in your surroundings to make the easiest thing first. Of course, the situation dictates. If you need protection from the rain or heat or snow, cold, and wind, then do what you need, but just past the minimum is what I recommend the first night. You will have plenty of other things to do.

- **The Time Factor:** Give yourself at least one hour to make a minimal shelter if you have good stuff around you. If there's not much around, give yourself two hours. Shelters take time to build. If it's early morning, great, you have time; if it's afternoon or evening, move shelter higher on the priority list. Even if you have something for shelter already, get in it and test it before dark.

  I have also taken all day to make a very good shelter, but only after I had food and water sorted out. With every shelter, be sure to gather lots of cushion for sleeping and lots of leaves and foliage to cover yourself for warmth.

  On Day One, you need only to create a shelter that's just good enough. Otherwise, hydrate, eat, keep dry, tend wounds, make fire, make tools, make signals, or do anything productive if there is plenty of daylight once you've made the shelter.

- **Otherwise, Sleep!** Sleep as much and as long as you can the first night. Start by getting rest, or "recovery." It is necessary for your machine, your body, to have down time to recover its strength and maintain its health. Do not underestimate the power of sleep to do this, and do not neglect it as a mandatory part of your planning in all phases.

- **Stay or Go?** After you've rested you can make a more informed decision to stay or go. If you decide to go, then having spent too much time on a shelter would have been a waste of time and energy.

  If you do decide to stay at your location, you might find your actual shelter site might not be the best one available in your immediate vicinity. So, **scout**! If you're staying put, scout around and see what you have available. If you decide you need to go, as you walk, always be on the look-out for a good shelter.

Bottom line, the function of a shelter is to protect you from the elements when necessary, and to protect you while vulnerable during sleep. Its quality level will affect your sleep, which in turn will affect all your decisions, judgment, and reaction time.

Considerations for Shelters

- **The Basics.** First of all, let me say that there is no exact "right way" to build a survival shelter. You will be making your shelter out of the materials available to you, and so each shelter you build will look different. However, there are basic principles that you should know and practice that will enable you to make fine protective shelters in practically any environment, regardless of what tools or resources you may or may not have. Some terms describing the most basic shelters include A-frame (a stick frame shaped like the letter "A"), tepee (shaped like a common Native American tepee and made from sticks and foliage), and lean-to (basically, a wall of sticks built on a leaning angle to protect from elements). You can also burrow out a shelter, make a shelter from rocks or logs, dig into snow, and so on. Let's get into the details. . . .

- **Get Off the Ground.** The first rule in all cases, really, is to get off the ground. I always look to the trees for shelter first when I need shelter fast. It gets me off the ground and keeps me safe from most things—flash floods, mean beasties, and bad bugs.

In a worst-case scenario where you have no tools or little time, simply find two good branches—one to sit on, straddle, or otherwise hold you up, with another one close enough to wedge yourself in so you won't fall out. And then let the rest of your body lean against the base of the tree. I call this "airplane sleeping." You're high up, and you can almost sleep, but not quite, like in the economy seats on airplanes.

But it will get you off the ground, provide you some shelter (if it's bushy enough, and not too windy or rainy), and it is safer than nothing unless you're so high that a fall would be harmful or fatal. In any case, it's wise to use a belt or shoe strings or an extra item of clothing to "tie in" so you don't fall completely.

■ **Building a Tree Shelter.** When picking a tree or trees, I first look to see if it is easy in and out, or in this case up or down. Try to find an easily climbable tree with a nice fork of two very strong branches and lay some other branches between them as a

Platform of sticks built between lower boughs of three trees

Tree shelter

platform—and a pretty good start point for a shelter. It helps to lash these branches down before building up on them. Look for a nice third branch as a roof center-piece.

If I'm among trees that are simply too big, look for smaller trees, ideally three or four close enough together that you can lay some other branches across their branch joints near the base to give a platform off the ground.

Once I build my bed frame, and the slats for the bed frame, I put down lots of soft bushy stuff for my mattress, actually about two-feet thick. I then fashion a roof in the same manner. The main concepts for the tree shelter are that it's off the ground, you have a strong platform, and there's a decent overhead cover.

- **Swamp Bed.** A swamp bed is like the tree shelter, except you create the legs by hammering three or four logs into the ground and then creating a platform frame on those. Unless you have incredible tools or amazing strength to drive the log-legs sufficiently into the ground, they will give way and you end up on the ground.

Ground-based shelter

- **Ground-Based Shelter.** Once you've got the platform laid out, start to fashion walls and a roof— IF you have the time, energy, and materials available. (You can just sleep right on the ground platform if necessary.)

The A-frame is simple to make. Start by angling two long branches from the ground up (about three to five feet apart), meeting at a center point a few feet off the ground, and lash them together, creating what looks like the letter "A." This is the front end of the frame where you

A-frame shelter

get in. Then make another "A" for the back of the shelter. Then lash one end of a long thick stick to the top of one A, and the other end to the top of the other A, and you've got the basic structure. Lay many sticks on an angle from this top beam down to the ground on either side then cover with as much foliage as you can find.

- **On, Not In.** *On* the ground is typically better than *In* the ground for numerous reasons. First, if it rains, you likely won't be flooded out. Second, creepy crawlies just seem to find holes in the ground. Next, the ground is colder and more wet if you dig into it.

- **In, Not On.** If it is excruciatingly hot or cold, try to get into the ground.

   If you are in a desert area that is all sand dunes, be exceedingly frugal with all energy and make conservative decisions. The key is to save water, so, dig into the sand to get to a little cooler spot and then use something to shade you from the sun.

   In cold mountains environs, like mountains or forest, look for areas covered in snow to dig a cave. Just digging into the snow and burrowing in will be surprisingly warmer than the outside air around you. Also try to put something between you and the snow.

   If there isn't enough snow to burrow into, but there is some, then try to fashion it into some form of shelter, like an igloo or a couple walls with sticks and branches on top. I've found igloos are hard to make without a snow shovel to cut nice blocks. But you can make large snowballs, place them as you would bricks, and then fill in the holes and gaps with snow and pack it in. I find a pyramid or simple mound shape like a quinzee hut shape works best because, as you stack your walls, each one a little closer in, the last row of snowballs will make your roof.

- **Time to Act.** Shelters take time, 1-4 hours often. Always ask: What could go wrong? Can I do this in a better way? Do I really need to do this at all, or are there other options? When you have time, take time!

  Now, if you don't have time, then make a decision and go hot! Often in urgent circumstances, where time is not an option, some decision is better than no decision.

- **Think about "SITtiNG."** This is another handy acronym that relates to survival shelters, and it makes sense since "sitting" is something you'll be doing a lot of inside it—thinking, working, planning, doing, and making things.

  "S" is for "shelter." Always find, build, and use one based on your environment.

  "I" is for "improvise." Use wreckage if available, and improvise all other materials from what's around you.

  "T" is for "trees." Always look to trees for shelter, whether as a quick sleep spot, as a frame with two or three trunks, or in a cluster.

  "N" is for "nature." Use all that nature provides, including caves, holes, logs, fallen trees, ditches, boulders, foliage, dirt, rocks, and so on.

  "G" is for "ground." Make a platform on the ground at least, as a last resort, and go underground in extremes.

Now let's look at typical survival shelters in specific environments.

Jungle

The best types of shelters are the store-bought kind. Of course, if you're in an unplanned survival situation, you won't have this. The concept is that these set the standard for you to strive for as you go about improvising your own shelter in the jungle environment.

Tents simply are not a good idea in real jungle as it's hard to find a clear, level, dry place to put one down. Any rain or critters pose more of a hazard to tent shelters as well. Best to think hammock and get off the ground.

But when it comes to jungle survival, I find old-fashioned is best. I go for the jungle trio "HiPiN" (Hammock, Poncho, Net)—and I prefer these to be separate units. For hammocks, I prefer the old-fashioned US Army jungle hammock. Not because it's the best; in fact, I often get a snag or button caught in the netting during the night. But I prefer them for their multipurpose utility. I can make them into a rucksack for carrying things or a litter for a wounded person or a trap for animals or a net for larger fish. They just make a good generic tool for a lot of uses. But I mostly use them as a bed, as opposed to the "survival" nets which can be used for everything and a bed, but they don't make the best bed, as they're not primarily a bed. Best to have a true bed that can also do other things than to have a multi-purpose tool that serves as a bed secondarily.

I also like my rain fly to be separate. Again, I prefer the US Army poncho. The reason is the same as with the hammock: I can use it as a poncho for shelter against wind, rain, and sun; I can make a raft or a huge water-catcher with it; I can use it to smoke meat; and any number of other uses.

The general rule in survival packing and planning is to get the most use for the least weight and space.

Most of the expensive specialty items that are designed for one specific thing offer less practicality when surviving, as the basic day-to-day needs of a human require many implements to fulfill. Therefore, your best tools are those you can rely on to handle a variety of jobs.

If I'm going to take the time to buy, pack, and carry stuff, I want to make sure I really get all I can out of it. And so it goes with my mosquito net. I like a separate mosquito net as I can use it in so many ways. Besides being a must-have item for sleeping, it can be used as a bird trap or a fish net. Sometimes you can get enough tiny minnows in them to make a nice simple meal all by itself.

- **Jungle Shelter without Gear.** Now if you don't have any gear, it gets back to the beginning on shelters—take to the trees.

The **swamp bed** comes to mind here. But the smart way is the easiest way that works. Don't bother with the classic method of making a swamp bed described above. Instead, take three smaller sticks/logs about one-foot long each, hold them in a bundle, and tie them with cordage (shoe string, ripped cuffs off your pants, natural material, whatever is available) and make one lash and a granny knot. When securely fastened, open the sticks like a tripod and place them down on the ground. Make four tripods and you got a swamp bed stand that you can take with you. These will set on the ground sturdily, no force needed, and they're easy to adjust as well. Once the four tripods are down, lay two long "poles" (branch, limb, thin log, etc) lengthwise onto the tops of the tripods, and two shorter poles as your width, and then lay slats, and then lay foliage to lay on and under.

Swamp bed

As for the lashings needed to put this all together, if you have no manmade cordage available, find some flexible vines, or pliant young sapling branches, or tough longer roots of small trees or plants, and wrap them into bundles; these should hold as a temporary lashing. It all takes a bit of feeling it out, but that's what it takes.

If you have nothing, and it's dark, or you're zapped of energy, you can always grab a few large-leafed plants and make a sort of blanket over yourself while leaning against the dry side of a tree. Try to find a tree that rises on a bit of an angle, and always look above for loose branches that may fall. Be sure and lay a lot of foliage underneath you for that ever-important elevation, and you'll make it through the night.

- **The Benefits of Bamboo.** Bamboo has to be the all-time best thing growing out there in nature. Not only can you make a bed or shelter from bamboo, you can also make utensils, weapons, canteens, pots, pans, cups, and more— you can even **eat** it! It's even great for starting fires.

One of the coolest uses of bamboo is to make a rain-gutter roof. To do this, split a number of bamboo shafts in half, and lay them all tightly together with the curved part facing up. The shafts should be vertical to the ground; not horizontal. Then lay other halves on top so that one edge is sitting in the groove of the upward facing pieces on either side. This make a wonderful waterproof roof in that most of the rain is blocked by the bamboo and then caught in the upward facing cups of the first row, allowing the water to run down to the edge.

It's important to make the roof plenty long so that the rain falls off the edge far enough away from you. I prefer a lean-to type roof as they're faster and easier to build. I make it at least two feet more around the edges than I need, and have it sloping downward in whatever I think is the best direction to block the rain and make it long enough to provide protection over your fire as well.

If it's rainy season, and you'll be holing up for awhile at your site, best to make an A-frame roof with your bamboo,

Bamboo roof with gutter

and lay one long fat piece of bamboo across the top to keep the rain from coming down the middle. You should also consider improvising a gutter to channel rain away from you and into some water-holding vessel. Even if it's just a hole you scraped out with a stick and then line with leaves to make a reservoir, it's a good way to save water and energy.

Desert

It can be scorching hot, freezing cold or even snowing. There can be long periods of drought, and then a sudden flash flood. So, the first thing to do in the desert is to get rid of any preconceived notions of what it is or isn't. The desert can kill you quick if you're disrespectful.

There will likely be some sort of physical terrain that will give you shade for a period of the day—find it and use it. In the middle of the day when the sun is at its blazing hottest, if you can't find any natural cover, then sit down, take off your clothes and use them to create a shade above yourself. If you can find or make a hole or depression to get into, then use your clothes as a cover above you.

If you do have a tarp, use it as a shelter during daytime. Place it a few feet above you to allow more heat to radiate off of it. If you have two covers, use one as the sun shield higher up, and the other a few inches under it to create a space that will trap heat while you remain remarkably cool underneath.

Desert shelter

However, this can be difficult if you don't have enough lashings and poles to keep your cover in place.

At night in the desert, expect the temperature to drop dramatically. If your overall plan includes trying to walk toward safety wherever it may be, then you may consider doing your traveling at night to avoid the heat of the day.

If you need to sleep at night, then be sure to scout a good location long before dark, and to gather the materials that will keep you warm. Small caves, the underside of rock ledges, thick brush, and other natural formations can serve as cover or shelter.

Arctic

When you're in the Arctic, or any sub-zero climate for that matter, the first order of business is to get out of the cold as soon as possible.

If you can find a field or cluster of rocks, seek shelter in them. There will likely be good pockets of space between the snow and rocks, and they'll block the wind better than trees can. If there are no such rock resources, get into the trees. Often there is space under the snow-covered tree boughs that make for a really nice, ready-made snow den.

If the snow isn't deep enough, then use the tree as temporary shelter for breaks from the wind as you build up a snow or debris wall. But even debris shelters take a lot of time and energy to make, so plan on the time to make even this simplest of shelters.

The simplest and quickest technique of getting out of the cold in an arctic or snow-

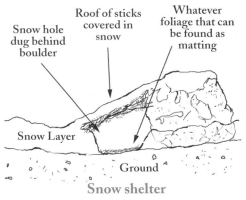

Snow hole dug behind boulder

Roof of sticks covered in snow

Whatever foliage that can be found as matting

Snow Layer

Ground

Snow shelter

covered area is simply to dig into the snow and cover up. It is remarkably warmer inside a snow cave, even a small one that you quickly dig out.

Ultimately, anytime you are stuck in a sub-zero environment, trying to stay and wait might not be your best option unless you have materials to sustain yourself for a long wait or you are fairly confident that a search party will be looking for you.

Seashore/Island

The seashore is usually an easier environment for survival. You can pretty much get all you need in most cases on the seashore. There is always debris floating up on the shore that can be used to make a shelter.

When you choose to build a shelter, always first look up to ensure that nothing is above you that might fall on you. Study the ground near your potential shelter location, looking for grooves in the ground that could have been made by flash floods, animal tracks, and tidal movement.

Leaves woven into slats

Leaves and branches found near beaches are usually great for making a shelter. Look for t "elephant ears," like taro plants. If not around, reach for palm fronds or any other large-leafed plants. Round palm fronds work well just as they are; other elongated fronds work better if split down the middle. All require a stick structure with slats, such as a lean-to, tepee, A-frame, etc. to build upon. If you have time, weave the leaves into the slats for extra sturdiness and weather protection. When there is no time to do so, simply lay enough slats to hold the leaves without falling through, and then lay a few more slats over all the leaves to give them security in bad weather.

Woodlands

In most woodlands there are many branches on the ground that still retain a lot of their original sturdiness and, unlike the tropics, they have not been corroded by the fast-decaying climate. The vegetation in woodlands is easier to deal with than jungles, as it doesn't grow as thick. In woodland survival is there isn't a real need to get off the ground; therefore the logistics are quite simple. Just lean some sticks together in an A-frame or teepee structure, or construct a basic lean-to, or use a tree as a lean-to, and start stacking pine boughs, various leaves, etc.

If it's still daylight after you've made your shelter, perform a quick "sun-spot check." Just lay inside your

shelter and look up, and if you can see any sunlight, that's an area that will be susceptible for rain to come in—so quickly fill those spots

Woodland shelter

in with more debris. You can also do a similar leak-check by building a small, safe fire in your hooch and look for smoke leaks coming out. With the smoke-check technique, you'll have the added benefit of repelling bugs.

Mountains

Mountain-area shelters are about the same as the woodlands, except you might incorporate boulders as walls against which you can fashion your lean-to. You may also find clusters of boulders to be your walls and you'll just need to make a roof and fill in any gaps in your walls with brush and branches.

Stone and stick tepee shelter

If there are no boulders to work with, there will likely be plenty of stones or rocks you can stack to make a good wall. Another technique is to make a shape of stones—square, circular, or triangular—simply piled one or two high. Then use them as a form against which you can wedge your sticks and make a nice little shelter.

Often a fallen tree or log can be found in the mountains, and these make a nice starter structure for a shelter, or even a good self-contained temporary shelter if you're wounded or too ill or depleted to make a shelter in time. Just pull up some soil or debris for coverage and get as comfortable as possible.

In fact, whenever you're building a shelter, make use of all your effort. What I mean is, when you dig up dirt or break apart sticks or rip up leaves, there will be debris from that activity. Use that debris! Put it to use by forming it into a small wall around your shelter, or as an insulator to keep out bugs, or as a stopgap to prevent leaks of water and wind, or as a small rain ditch around any ground shelter. The basic idea is to use all resources available in your situation, and to maximize all your efforts.

Another trick to handling rain is to tie a piece of string where it is entering and angle it so the water will be diverted away from you. Or, for the edges of a roof or the top joint of an A-frame, have your foliage overlap a good six inches or more so that the rain is dispersed long before it gets to the joint and then flows down the side walls instead of dripping into the middle of your home. If despite all that, it still rains into your hooch, dig a little channel and direct it out the door and sleep on the opposite side. You've got nothing better to do but home improvement in these cases, or conduct personal hygiene and take a bath instead!

Swamp

The swamp can be pretty tough going. If you get stranded there, be prepared for a mental battle as it can be very intimidating as you're frequently submerged, which reduces your body temperature and softens the skin, which increases exposure to damage and infection. Also, swamps are often filled with gators and snakes. However, like the jungle, mountains, or island settings, one can survive there a long time—unlike the desert and Arctic. But the chances

Swamp platform shelter

of being found in a swamp are extremely slim unless a plane wreck left a good imprint in the ground. Even then, the marsh usually just swallows these up and the traces of a wreck are very hard to find for rescuers. So, staying in the swamp is not a real good plan. What that means here is that you don't really want to spend a lot of time making a shelter here. Therefore, swamp shelters should be the minimum needed to get through the night, and then you should continue moving by day unless you're ill or injured.

The ultimate rule of swamp shelters is to seek high ground. Often you'll find small patches of drier, harder ground to make a shelter on. It's still good to get off the ground even if it is harder, it will often moisten very quickly as you work around your site and turn into quite a muddy mess. If you can get off the ground, take extra care and time to stack a very high pile of grass and padding to keep you dry at the top.

In these cases, start early and make a swamp bed. Forget the method of driving poles into the ground, and instead tie into some trees. The ground here is often so wet and sloppy, it's pure foolishness to try making a platform of sticks stabbed into the boggy ground.

Again, like the nest platform described earlier, chop or break some strong branches, lay them into the forks formed by branches of a closely grouped set of standing tree branches, and build a platform to get you up out of the water. Hang everything off the trees around you to dry while you rest, and do all you can to keep yourself dry as well.

Once you have a platform constructed to hold you up and get you out of the water, try to fashion a roof over your structure in case it rains. But if you don't think it necessary, don't spend the time on a roof. The platform alone will take longer than you think. Again, the key is that you won't be staying long and therefore, it's more like a roadside motel instead of a nice vacation resort. Just get dry, get rest, and then get moving.

Urban

The first priority tends to be shelter in terms of staying hidden from anyone who might be a threat. Warehouses, abandoned buildings or vehicles, particularly trucks and trailers, are good places. Containers and dumpsters can be if they're not in a highly populated area. The main thing is to be sheltered from harm by remaining unseen.

A significant factor here will be time. If unfriendly people will be looking for you, you don't have time and so you must make a movement. Or if you don't think anyone is coming to your rescue, you don't have time and must make a movement. Either way, you may have to move around often and find various shelters until you can make a movement out of the urban environment and start living off the land.

There are a few key elements to consider for urban shelters:

How much space it gives you to loiter and rest during daylight, as you'll likely be making any movements at night.

Does a shelter offer an escape route, or would it become a death trap if the entrance was blocked?

Are you able to eat, drink, and utilize the latrine, if there is one, without compromise?

The fact is you won't be constructing anything, but rather, you'll be exploiting objects based on availability and isolation. We've all seen hobos and homeless folks turn boxes into homes, and newspapers into beds, and the tools of their trade is good stuff in urban survival.

Also, think about all the places to hide in plain sight. Overpasses, railroads, bushes in the middle of a highway exit ramp, even sewers and under houses are good places to hole up for the day. You can even sleep in the row of bushes outside of a mall or corporate building as everyone is so busy there during the day, they never think to suspect someone might be hiding in the bushes in broad daylight right in the public view.

Sewers are rough and smell, but they have the advantage of being overlooked by most, and you can discreetly track what's going on around you, and often you'll have an egress route.

The other thing I have learned is that dogs and kids will always find you. When looking for a hide site, the exact places we seek are the same things kids look for in order to play. Likewise, if you're close enough to people, you'll be close enough for their pets, and pets are always sniffing around for places to defecate or urinate.

In plain sight will serve you right; public too near, much to fear.

Two of the most important factors for urban improvised shelters are to always have an egress or escape route, and to set up early-warning alarm systems by placing bottles or twigs or leaves or gravel around your sleeping area. This way, if anyone happens to walk near you, they will make a crunch or other noise to wake you. At that point you have to decide whether to utilize your egress, or freeze and wait. Often the sound will distract them, too, and they'll be less inclined to notice you.

3

WATER

I like to break down the basics of water into a few simple rules.
1. Keep it in you.
2. Get it in you and keep it flowing in.
3. If you have it, ration it. If not, prioritize the gettin' of it.
4. Scan around for water sources such as flows, holes, cracks, and traps.
5. Use plants, animals, bugs, and birds before working for it yourself.
6. Scout hard before walking long; look hard before digging. Never dig too deep, and consider digging more than one hole.
7. Combine digging, plants, and other options and tricks when there is no obvious answer.
8. Use all your wits when you have nothing else to go on.
9. Break all the rules when all else fails.

WHAT YOU REALLY NEED, AND HOW TO USE IT

Everyone starts off by saying a lot about what you need. I'm gonna start by talking about what you don't need.

You don't need as much as you think and you certainly don't need as much as you drink back home. Fact, humans have mostly lived throughout history at a very low level of hydration, yet, we're still here. So we don't need as much as modern standards suggest, but you must get *some* fluids in you or the harsh fact is that you will die.

People have about five liters of blood in their body. The heart pushes this amount from any start point to the same finish point in one minute. About 60-100 beats per minute, about 12-16 breaths per minute.

On average about one liter of water can be lost each day, just by laying there and breathing.

Add to that any complications such as high heat, high humidity, extreme cold making the body work harder to stay warm, loss of blood through trauma, less than optimal functioning and therefore inefficient use of water in the body already due to illness or fatigue (which is to be expected in the stress of any survival scenario), and it is easy to see how dehydration can set in very quickly.

The human body starts to lose effectiveness with a simple decrease of only ½ liter of blood volume since the average total body composition is about 60% water. A mere loss of only 2% causes overall performance to deteriorate. A 4% loss leads to muscle capacity decreasing; 6% leads to heat exhaustion; 8% leads to hallucinations;

and loss of 10% of body fluid can cause circulatory collapse, stroke, and death.

Most people do not drink enough water daily to begin with, so they are already operating at a deficit when the survival scenario commences.

What all this means is, unless you happen to have plenty of water, then water needs to be one of your very first priorities. Right after life-saving first aid and shelter, water is right there or else survival won't be happening.

Do not become complacent because it is too hot or cold, etc. You must be very aggressive in your pursuit of water while you can, or heat stroke and dehydration can jump your bones before you realize it and then it's game over.

Let's look at what happens when you don't have water so you'll know what to be looking for and how to track your progress and status. However . . . I want you to remember to take all this in, and then throw it out. You'll see what I mean shortly.

The First Signs and Symptoms of Dehydration:
Thirst
Headache
Decreased urinary output
Dark strong-smelling urine, pain
Light-headedness, dizziness, or fainting when standing up from sitting or squatting (Postural Hypotension)

More Advanced Stages of Dehydration:
Lack of tears if crying
Rapidly fatigued (Lethargy)
Constipation and loss of appetite
Rapid heart rate (Tachycardia)
Elevated body temperature
Nausea and vomiting
Tingling in the limbs (Paresthesia)
Skin may become shriveled and wrinkly; pinching it may reveal reduced elasticity (Turgor)
Visual disturbances, hallucinations, delirium, unconsciousness and death.

For example, if you notice that you feel light-headed when you stand up, then you are already dehydrated.

So, know the signs and symptoms of dehydration as a check system for yourself, but do not get discouraged by any doctrine that states you only have so long to live or can't make it without a certain amount of water. Human beings have survived weeks without water. They have drank urine and lived. They have drank sea water and lived. They have eaten snow and lived. They have lost tremendous amounts of blood from trauma or electrolytes from disease and diarrhea and still lived; and so can you!

Ideally, one would drink 500ml every hour when it's hot or when doing strenuous exercise or very laborious work. That's one of the standard individual drinking water bottle sizes. It works out to about 10 hours of work a day, drinking 5 liters of water total, which is completely replenishing the full amount of blood volume. This is an ideal.

The reality is that we lose about 3-4 liters of water a day and we get most of that back every day, about 20% from our food and the other from the thirst generated by the food we ate and then slaked by quenching that thirst.

However, in extreme circumstances, if you can get just one 500ml bottle's worth of fluid in you each day you can survive. Even if you only get 100ml, that is something, and can help keep you hanging in there.

Whether you get this from your environment, from cacti, fish eyes, frozen ice being melted next to your skin, another source, or from what small amounts of water you have already that you're rationing, then your approximate number of survival days is roughly equal to the number of 500ml life-giving water infusions you have or can make available.

That is, provided one is not ill or injured, and is working with their environment in as smart a manner as possible, and the daily physical workload isn't much more than standing and walking. Using what you have—and keeping it inside you—is the key to success, when you don't have enough water.

Working smarter is the way ahead. Pace your work so you don't sweat. Try to pace yourself in all survival situations so that you don't rush and make mistakes, but also so you don't sweat and lose water.

Sweat happens when you push the machine and it needs to cool down. It's a mechanism that allows the body to push hard and still keep cool. But when sweat is precious life-water draining your very chance of survival drop by drop, try to work at a comfortable pace so that the work is still being accomplished but the sweat is not wasted. Best to keep it in you is the golden rule.

When it comes to hardcore immediate survival, food is simply not an important issue initially so forget about it, but make water one of your almighty priorities.

How Much Time You Have

Now here are the harsh facts. If you're seriously dehydrated, diseased, have terrible diarrhea, have lost lots of blood, had been partying hard the night before you got stuck in this situation and have a bad hangover, and you're in the middle of the desert in the summer time . . . realistically, you only have about 24 hours to live.

If you're ok in all the above categories but you're still in the desert in summer, without water, you realistically only have about three days.

And in an ideal situation, with some water and some know-how, in the desert in summer, you might have about seven days.

These are your approximate timelines for survival in a desert region. They basically apply in the sea as well, since that is also one of the harshest environments to survive without water. They don't really apply to the Arctic as you can eat the snow. Everyone says not to do so, but that is crap. The reason they say not to is because it reduces your core temperature, which is true. But if you have dry clothes and a shelter and can basically maintain warmth, without a fire, then there is no reason to die of dehydration when surrounded by good water in the form of snow.

Now, these are only approximations to help you make the best strategies for how you work, build a shelter, and maneuver yourself in your environment. If you factor these in, and operate accordingly, you can extend these timelines indefinitely.

Knowing you only have seven days in the desert with a small amount of water, will help dictate to you if you need to risk a movement or if you can afford to hold and wait for rescue. But all the hope and willpower in the world will not change the fact that you will need some water sooner or later, so plan on getting it or using what you have to get you out.

First Priority in Finding Water

Water technique 1
Plastic bag placed over foliage will yield water

The first place to start looking is where you are and in what you have.

Is there water around you? Look for a river, stream, lake, creek, pond, water fountain, fish tank, toilet, flower pot, kettle, water tank on the roof of a building, and anywhere around you naturally or manmade.

Next, look at the environment's indirect potential water sources: snow, ice, rain, fog, morning dew, puddles, etc.

If nothing directly or indirectly water-producing is available, start by looking right where you are as many folks end up in a survival situation while in transit on some form of transportation. Is there any water in your craft, vessel, or vehicle. Look first in all the obvious places—storage spaces, emergency compartments, maybe things that were left behind or stowed away and forgotten.

When all the immediate ideas do not produce or stops producing, start to

Water technique 2
Water off large leaves after rainfall

Water technique 3
Melting ice or snow near a fire

think outside the box. If your natural and manmade resources are lacking, it's time to start looking at the alternatives and techniques that can get you water without digging.

Start looking at the environment for anything that might serve as catchment for water. Rock crevices, holes, cracks, plants with pockets or pools of water that might be trapped at joints, the base of stalks, the splits in trees, or anything around you that may contain small pools of water.

Water technique 4
Wiping dew off a cold surface

Making Water Safe to Consume

There are many ways to make water safe to drink, and water from any unknown source, natural or manmade, should be made safe to drink **always**.

Of course, if there is simply no way to make found water safe, and you can find no other source, then the choice is simple: drink it and *maybe* die, or don't drink it and *surely* die.

- **Boil It** The best way to make sure your water is 100% safe is to boil the heck out of it for 10 minutes. This is what most books and experts say, and that's groovy *if* you happen to have enough firewood for sustaining the fire that long. It's also time consuming, as it takes a while to get the fire going, boil the water, drain it and/or let it cool so you can drink it, and then, really, it's time to begin again.

So, ideally, do 10 minutes of boiling if you have a pot and fuel. If you have less tinder or time, drop it down to five minutes, unless it's really muddy, dirty water.

If scant fuel is available, a full one minute at a rolling boil will do the trick most of the time and, in fact, this is all I ever do. But in a real bind for a heat source, just get it hot enough to hit a boil and most likely it will be ok, but it will be safer than before anyway.

- **Treat It with Chemicals** Ideally, one can use any of the multitude of fancy chemical tablets and liquids out there that are designed to make the water safe to drink.

  The survivor rarely has access to these store-bought chemicals, so let's look at some improvised ways to treat water chemically.

  Bleach is great as it's found all over the world and it's easy to use. There are many formulas out there for how much to use, but I try to keep everything simple and use the "P for Plenty" formula as long as it's safe. Basically, a spoonful per gallon won't hurt you.

Rule for Adding Bleach to Cleanse Water:
1 drop of 10% strength for a liter
10 drops of 1% strength per liter
5 drops of 10% strength for a gallon
10 drops of 1% strength for a gallon
Double all amounts above if the water is especially dirty
Add the bleach, shake vigorously, let set for 15-30 minutes, then drink up. Most people drink some chlorine in their tap water every day, so it is safe.

Bleach will kill a lot, and though it won't kill all giardia, it sure will put a hurt on it and if it's all you got, go hot.

Iodine is also a great way to treat your drinking water. The thing is that it takes longer, so allow it to sit about 30 minutes to do its work, or double that time it if it's very cold.

This is why I keep liquid iodine drops in my first aid kit. It not only can treat a minor cut when you don't have water to wash it out, but it also doubles as a way to treat water and make it safer to drink.

Most Tincture of Iodine comes in a dark glass bottle of 2% strength. You need to place a few drops into your water and shake, then let stand for 30 minutes before consuming.

Rule for Cleansing Water with 2%-Strength Iodine:
2 drops per 1 liter
10 drops per gallon

■ **Filter It** There are many store-bought filters which can be used and should be used whenever possible and available. Usually they are not handy, and some sort of filtration method is better than nothing to get rid of at least the big bugs and other debris.

Layers of material can best filter water. Try to use a couple of socks, pant legs, a few scarves tied to a tripod of sticks—anything to form a set of shelves through which to flow the water. Or use anything else you may have or can find, such as a gallon jug with the bottom cut off and turned upside down with the lid off to filter it through.

Once you have your shelves set (if you can only make

one layer of shelf, so be it), then use whatever natural materials you have available to filter the water through; think of a charcoal filter.

You can use sand, loam, rocks, dirt, charcoal from your fire, or other such materials to filter your water. The key here is to use the biggest stuff at the top and make layers down to the finest stuff at the bottom. Also be sure to use your finest cloth at the bottom to keep the smallest particles from draining into your container.

If you have a lot of water, like a stream, it's good to run the water though this a few times to drain out and dilute any particles, bad flavors, or odors.

Water filter

This method of filtering will not kill or remove giardia, but it will make the water smell and taste better and reduce the overall bacteria load.

■ **Strain It** When you really have nothing, and you can't afford to be cutting up your clothes to make a temporary filter for what amounts to just about a luxury item anyway, sometimes it's just best to use Mother Nature as your strainer with the water hole.

Dig a water hole near the water source and let that hole fill in. Then drink up. Dig about one foot or so from the river or pond to dig your hole about one foot.

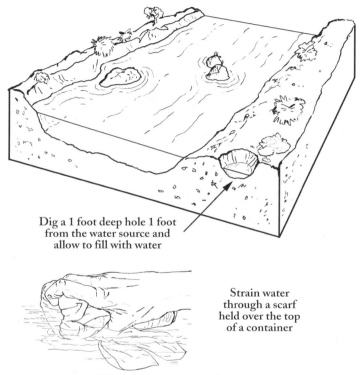

Dig a 1 foot deep hole 1 foot from the water source and allow to fill with water

Strain water through a scarf held over the top of a container

Water-straining techniques

■ **Sun It** When you have no way to boil, layer, filter, or otherwise treat your water, you can let the sun do the work for you. The light from the sun comes in the form of UV rays and can make your water safe.

A clear plastic bottle is ideal, but anything that is clear can be used, even a ziplock bag or piece of plastic. Only use about four inches of water, as any more is difficult for the UV rays to penetrate.

Take the water you have, filter it to get the sun-blocking particles out. Put the water in the cleanest, clear plastic or glass container you have, nearly fill it, shake it well to oxygenate it, then top it off so that no air space is left.

Then, leave it in the sun for as long as you can. Lay it on something black or hot like a dark rock or metal surface to help increase the heat. The hotter it gets, the better. The longer in the sun it remains, the better.

Basic Guidelines for Sunning Water:
On a hot day, the water can get over 120 degrees (the target temp) in about an hour
If it's sunny and warm but not hot, it will take about six hours
If it's not that hot, but bright and sunny, it can take 12 hours, or all day
If it's consistently cloudy, then let it sit for two full days
The one problem with this technique is that the bacteria will build back up, unlike when you boil water which makes it safe for storage for awhile. So, in all sun conditions, it's best to set your bottle(s) out in the morning and drink the water when the time is right. In other words, you pretty much have to drink what you treat each day.
But the bottom line, you can make your water safer to drink just by putting it in the sun. As a last resort for sunning water, even a bucket or other container with the water exposed to the sun can do some good; just sip the water off the top after it's been exposed for a period of time.

- **Just Dew It** A great simple way to get some water is to collect dew in the morning hour. The simplest method here is to use all the clothing you have and wipe it all over the grass, plants, and foliage on trees. Just walk through the thick fields of grass at the first light of the morning with scarves and tee shirts tied around your ankles to catch all the dew, then squeeze the water into your mouth or container.

- **Worst-Case Scenario: Enema** In medicine, when faced with severe cases of dehydration and when IV access is not available, a method for consuming water that has been around a long time is to use an enema. If you have water and it's not clean, you will have use an enema to get it in you.

Keys to Finding Water

- **Plants** All kinds of plants can help you find water and tell you when it's bad. If you find what looks like a stagnant pool, look for the plant life—if it's void of any, steer clear. If plants are thriving there, chances are good the water is okay.

- **Animals** They can help you find a source of water in that most animals are as dependent on water as humans are. This general rule doesn't apply so much to the meat eaters as they get some fluids from their prey, but they do need to drink after a kill. If you see a predator, take note of its direction of travel; if it has recently killed (look for blood), it might just be going toward a water hole.

  Look for game trails. Like with people, these will likely lead to a home or a hole. If you find such trails coming together, you're likely headed in the right direction to find small streams.

Finally, look for animal feces as a sign for water nearby.

Most animals need water regularly, and so they drink every day, usually at morning and evening. So, this is the best time to take note of your surroundings, study what is going on, and look for the critters to talk to you. They can show you the way to their favorite drinking spot, and yours.

- **Insects** Bugs can also help you find water. Flies tend to always stay within 100–200 meters, bees generally stay within five miles of a water source. Ants tend to form lines leading to water catchments likes trees or plants. Mosquitoes often breed in or around water.

- **Birds** If you are on land, and you see small grain-eating birds flying in the morning or evening, they are often heading to or from a water source. Especially if they are flying fast and low in a general direction as a group, then they are headed for water. If they are moving in short sort of hops from tree to tree, they have just likely come from a water hole.

- **Clouds** These can sometimes help you to find water as well. If it rains or looks like it, *stop everything* and *use everything* to catch all the water you can.

Also, take off your clothes and get a wash (hygiene is still important when you're surviving, but more on that later). Use your clothes to catch water and wring it into a container or your mouth if you have nothing else. Make a hole if you don't have any leaves or poncho or tarp or cups or jugs. Catch, drink, and repeat as long as it's pouring down.

If you're out to sea or in a remote place like the desert, clouds can indicate a possible water source if they are hovering in the same area for a long time.

How to Find Water in Specific Ecosystems

Desert

The desert is the classic worst-case scenario for survival. Most deserts do have plenty of life, and all life depends on water. The key is to know where to look and what to use.

■ **Scout.** First, follow the basic rules for locating water: scan the area, look for low-lying areas where water would converge and collect if it were flowing. Follow the natural lines of the terrain for the lowest points. Then look and see if there are plants and, if so, notice how green and healthy they appear. The greener the plant life, the more plentiful the water.

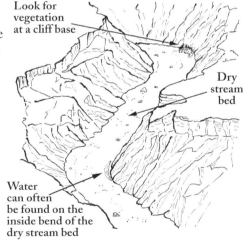

Look for vegetation at a cliff base

Dry stream bed

Water can often be found on the inside bend of the dry stream bed

Finding water sources

If you do find these low points with greenery, they are likely in some dry stream bed. Look for water first just to see if it's sitting there on the surface, then look at any walls of the gullies to see if there is some seepage of water on the face of the rocks.

If there is no open source, or no obviously wet or moist areas, then look for the bends in the dry river bed. The outsides of these bends will be where the water would have been the most recently, as it would have lasted there longest. Therefore, you might find some water there if you dig a bit.

But before you start digging, take a good look. If it looks bone dry, chances are there isn't any water there. So, calculate how much time, energy, and water you have on and in you, *before* you start prospectin' for water in the desert. Save the digging until you're sure, or you're desperate.

If the ground looks a bit moist, find the lowest point and dig about one foot down to start. If you dig two feet down and don't hit water, chances are, you're not gonna find any in that location. But don't give up yet; come back and check your holes later, maybe some water will have seeped in.

- **Collect Dew.** First, try to collect it off plants and grass if there are any about with dew on them. Then try flipping over some rocks to see if the cold air from the night had condensed as the sun rose and heated them; this will at least give you a bit of a wetness for your tongue.

Alternatively, you can try to make your own dew. Dig a hole about two feet around and about one foot deep, line it with a small piece of plastic (if you don't have plastic, use desert plants like the flat cacti that can keep moisture partially retained), and lay some rocks in the hole overnight. Make sure you wipe the rocks free of all dirt, debris, and sand first. In the morning, the rocks in the hole will have collected more dew than the surrounding exposed rocks, and you should get to lick a little off them.

- **Cacti and Plant Life.** The cactus is a good source of moisture in the desert. Notice I said moisture, not water. You have to chop them off and cut off the outside if they are the flat cacti; or if you've got barrel cacti, lop the top and chop up the insides. In both cases, get past the spikes and get the clean pulp into your mouth. The flat cacti are slimy, the barrel cacti are spongy, but they both will give you moisture. Suck out all the juice you can and spit out the pulp. Don't throw it away, use that for your solar still.

  The prickly pear is a nice fruit that grows on the tops of the flat cactus. They are tricky to de-skin as their spines are much finer than the cactus itself, but they are a deliciously sweet thing. I don't count them as a good source of water due to their sugar content, but if you're down to suckin' cacti, suck them too.

  The big agave plants that are common in many deserts sometimes have water trapped at the base of their meaty and pointy leaves, although these things are strong and the water is hard to get to.

- **Make a Solar Still.** Save all the ejected pre-sucked cacti bits and pieces and then use them to make a solar still. The solar still is one of the best friends of anyone surviving. The only catch is, without a poncho, tarp, or some sort of plastic, you can't make one.

  The concept of making a solar still is simple. Dig a hole about 1-2 feet deep minimum, or a bit deeper if you can do so without putting yourself in jeopardy by sweating too much. Make the hole as wide as your tarp, poncho, or plastic sheet will cover completely. In essence, you want a cone-shaped hole dug into the ground.

Then place a bunch of vegetation, spit-out cacti, bad water, even urine, and anything green in the hole. Now, place a cup or something to catch water in the center of the hole. Lay you tarp over the hole and use rocks or sand to secure its edges on the surface above the hole so that it's as air tight as possible. Then place a nice-sized, smooth, and as round a rock as you can find in the middle of the tarp outside the hole. This rock should force the tarp to droop slightly down into the hole above the water catch that's inside.

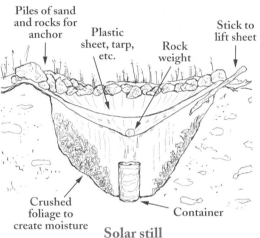

Piles of sand and rocks for anchor

Plastic sheet, tarp, etc.

Rock weight

Stick to lift sheet

Crushed foliage to create moisture

Container

Solar still

Now, here's how it works. The heat from the desert sun will draw all the moisture from all your materials inside the hole, and it will condense on the inside of the tarp. Then, gravity from the rock that's on the outside of your tarp will cause the water to trickle downward and drop into your cup. After a while, just raise the tarp gently, get the cup, drink it all, place it back, and then re-seal your still to keep it working.

Make as many of these stills as you have time and supplies.

Add urine, dirty water and any leafy green stuff you can find, but don't let it touch the edges of the tarp—keep it all flat by stepping on the plants a bit to bruise and crush them and get them oozing and leaking any moisture they have. (Any impurities will be distilled in the solar process.)

Be aware that a solar still won't fix you for the day, hydration wise. Usually, maybe 200-300 ml of water, or about maybe half a normal bottle of drinking water.

If you have plastic bags, you can try the evaporation method of placing the bag around as much foliage and vegetation as you can and tie it off on the open end and place a small pebble in a corner to weigh it down so all the water converges there.

The trick is to find leaves that appear light and green and not too thick or dark, and certainly not any that ooze white stuff if you break them. The water will be greenish in color, but it is fine.

Arctic

The arctic environment has plenty of water in the form of snow and ice, but this can kill you because consuming it will decrease your core body temperature, which will cause your body to shiver more to stay warm, which in turn will cause further dehydration. This is why it is strongly advisable to always melt snow or ice with fire before consuming it in water form.

Rules for Hydrating in Arctic Regions:
Snow and ice should be melted and boiled before drinking.
The best and most effective way to melt it is in a pot over a fire.
If you have no pot, wrap a ball of ice or snow in a t-shirt or other material, hang near fire and let it drip into a container.
If you have no cloth or pot or cup, try heating a rock in the fire and then melting snow or ice with it. First, dig a small hole and pack the inside walls of it tightly. Then drop in a soft pile of snow, and drop the heated rock on it. Once the snow has melted, quickly and safely remove the rock and sip out all the water.
If you need to draw water from sea ice, use the blue stuff— the bluer the better as it has less salt.
Make a hard-packed snowball and place it on a stick like a big marshmallow over a fire, but first have something to catch the water as it drips. If you don't have a catch, clean the stick as well as you can, and then let the water from the melting snowball drip down the stick into your mouth.

At Sea

The sea is one of the most desolate places for finding drinking water. If you don't have a desalinization kit or a reverse-osmosis pump, you're starting off with a serious challenge.

Otherwise, the best source of water when surviving at sea will come from the atmosphere. If it rains, drink all you can, catch all you can, store all you can. If you have fog, then use all the cloth you can to capture that and squeeze its moisture into a container or your mouth. Try to make a solar still.

You can also get some juice and hydration from fish. Fish eyes hold a very viscous fluid. Think of it as a jelly water. And some fish have water along their spiny area.

Seashore

If you're stranded on a small island with no dune break, then try to drop back past the highest watermark you can see and start digging a hole there. If there is vegetation, that is a good sign, as usually plants won't grow where the tide reaches.

If there are dunes, then drop back behind the first row of dunes and start digging.

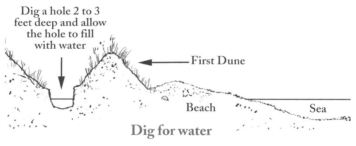

Dig a hole 2 to 3 feet deep and allow the hole to fill with water

First Dune

Beach   Sea

Dig for water

In both cases, the holes you dig will fill with water and this water will be safe enough to drink. Be prepared to dig a 2, 3 or even 6 foot-deep hole, and just as wide as the sand tends to fall back in. Use wood planks, to make a supporting wall to prevent the sand caving in on itself.

Once these holes fill, if you want to make the water a bit safer to drink, get a fire going, heat up some cleaned rocks, and place them in your pool of filtered sea water.

Often the seashore in the tropics will have coconuts. The coconut is a great source of water and food. The greener the nut, the better the water; the browner the nut, the more meat and white milk which will cause diarrhea if too much is drunk.

A word of caution: a coconut is a truly tough nut to crack without a blade. The best method I have seen is to shave down to the nut with a shell or rock, then use the outer shell as a way to hold the nut up so you can crack into it without spilling the juices everywhere. Another way is to make a sharp pointy stick and use it as a sort of spike-wedge. Stick the spike into the ground and stab the coconut onto it, then leverage the husk against the stick to de-husk it. Then use a rock, and tap the nut hard all around the sides. Often this will crack it in half and yield the fruit of your labor.

If it becomes your last resort, try sea water.

Hawke's Rules for Drinking Sea Water:

Don't do it unless you are sure you will die from dehydration; wait until it's absolutely desperate, and you realize there is no hope for finding water via fish, rain, or other means.

Start early if you know it's inevitable. If you are in the middle of the ocean and have no water at all, and there's no real hope of immediate rescue, your start point is after your first 24 hours without water.

Don't wait until it's too late, as you may start to go crazy from delirium caused by dehydration, and the salt will push you over the edge.

Dilute it if you can with any good water you may have, or take sips here and there in between rinses or swallows of your fresh water.

If you have the materials and are on a small vessel or floating device, make a solar still (as described on p.56).

Never, ever drink more than a few gulps of seawater at a time, and then never more than approximately a cup over a 24-hour period.

Ration small amounts of fresh water and space out the timing of consumption.

The bottom line is that drinking salt water from the sea is a bad thing, and shouldn't be done. But it can be done and should only be done when death seems very probable.

Jungle

The jungle is one of my personal favorite regions for surviving. A key element here is to always take the time to ask locals about what plants are good for water.

Water Vine

- **Water Vine.** There are many vines in the jungle. Not all provide water, but many do. It takes a bit of practice at first to identify them. Usually their bark is a bit lighter and fluffier than the non-water vines, and when you tap them, they sound more hollow than the white-sap-producing varieties. To get to the water, cut **high** then **low**. They suck the water up from the ground at the first cut (called "capillary action") so that if you cut low first, the water will be sucked up already by the time you cut high and you'll have less water to drink. They are fairly easy to cut through.

Hold the vine like a long canteen and let the water drain into your mouth. If you can get your fill and also have a container, fill up on all the water from vines you can find. The water tastes great, it's safe, and the vines are easy to cut. Without a knife, try to break it open high with a heavy stick, then break it low with your hands and/or with leverage over a branch and drink it that way.

There are some trees that have root systems similar to the water vine. They do not yield as much water, but a good drink can be had. Try to learn these before you go or if you have time and energy, then experiment by chopping some roots on two sides, and hold it up to drain, then, if you're lucky, give them a minute and they'll ooze pure drinking water.

Cut the trunk of the banana tree to fill with water

Banana or Plantain Tree

- **Banana (or Plantain) Plants.** This is a wonderful plant to find. It can be felled right across the base just like chopping a head of cabbage in half, and then, watch it fill. The water is good, though it's strong-tasting at first and mellows after a few bowlfuls. This plant will also generate water for awhile, so you might even camp there for a day or two if you find one.

- **Fig Tree.** It can give up a lot of water but needs to be tapped into. Use a piece of pipe, or tube, or some small bamboo fashioned into a tube, then cut a hole into the tree and wedge the tube in and let the water drain, but make a reservoir catch for it.

- **Palms.** Nipa, buri, coconut, and sugar. You can get water from many of these fruits, and even the little ones will yield a nice lemonade-flavored water. As well, you can draw water from the tree itself. Best to use the small ones 12 feet high or smaller so you can reach the top, chop it off, and keep it bent over so it will "bleed" water for you. This can be a repeated a few times to stimulate more sweet water production.

Bromeliad

■ **Leaves.** Bromeliads, pitcher plants, elephant ears, et al. Bromeliads are what I call "tree celery." They are sometimes called air plants, because they seemingly grow in the air (some they take root in pockets on a tree, like where a branch broke off; others grow in the soil that settled where a tree fell). Not only do these plants have a sort of lettuce quality in that they are smooth, but they're also crisp like celery and they trap water in the joints. Also, their leaves can be chewed like the white base of celery, and a good amount of tasty water will come from them.

The elephant ears (taro) or any big leaves should catch your attention for two reasons.

First, they might have some water trapped in them or at their base. Also, these large leaves make excellent devices for catching rainwater. Surround your camp with these rolled into cone shapes and then wedged into every tree branch around my hooch so they can catch and fill up with water during any rain.

- **Bamboo.** As stated before for different reasons (i.e. shelter building), bamboo is a gift from the gods in respect to water, as well. The green bamboo can be bent over and the top cut off to produce water; the older, browner ones usually have water trapped inside their segments. Tap or shake them and listen for the water swishing and splashing. If you hear that, cut a little notch at the base of each segment and drain the water. Usually, you can do this with each segment above and below as bamboo shoots are compartmentalized.

Bamboo

Pitcher Plant

- **Pitcher Plant.** This Southeast Asian plant looks just like a pitcher of water. It's usually filled with dead bugs and what not, but if you can boil or treat the water, it's a nice find.

- **Baobab Tree.** Found in Africa and Australia, the baobab holds large amounts of water in its trunk and is a true gift if you happen across one. They're easy to identify as they're super fat and funky looking.

- **Traveler's Tree.** This native of Madagascar has leaves with a cup at the base that catches and holds water. These are niceties, but not really worth planning for.

Mountains

Finding water in the mountains can be a challenge. Stay on the high ground, preferably the ridge line so you can look for land sloping down on both sides until you see a source of water. Then drop down towards it.

Remember: Walls and cliffs are the best secrets for looking for water in mountainous areas. Often these breaks in the integrity of the mountain range will have a leak from some small underground spring as it pushes through the mountain.

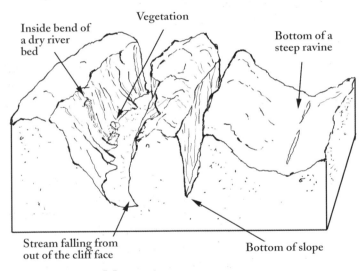

Mountain water sources

Forest

Find the lowest point you can. Usually, the higher and steeper the two hills are that create a ravine, the better the chances are of finding water. Find the greenest, wettest, lowest point you can and dig a hole 1- to 2-feet deep maximum. Give it awhile and see if any water seeps in. If not, try the condensation method described on page 56 using a poncho (or natural materials like leaves) to cover the hole, so your effort in digging it doesn't go to waste, then keep looking. If you're hunting for little trickles of water, the opposite holds true—a good, long, wide slope of a hill basically means more surface area to catch water and channel it down. Where willow and cottonwoods grow often indicates water. Anytime you step on some soggy soil, you're likely on a water source.

Swamp

The problem in swamps is making that water safe to drink. Fires can be a challenge to make. The strategies are: dig a filter hole, use your clothes and charcoal/sand, or scoop up some water into a shallow container and let the sun work on it for the day.

Urban

Surviving in a city that's under siege from a natural or manmade disaster is an often overlooked aspect of surviving. It is good to look for water near you and to start early. Areas to consider include parks, golf courses, drainage ditches, rooftop reservoirs, water cans in gardens, water hoses with water left inside, city water fountains found in parks, amusement parks, aquariums, farms or zoos or anywhere animals may be kept.

Know where the water sources are near your home, your work, and the routes to and from the places you go.

Last Resorts

You can drink urine! The rules for urine drinking are straightforward: drink it as soon after you urinate as possible; the first time you urinate is usually fine to drink; and you can drink the second pass in dire circumstances.

After the second pass, chances are that you won't be urinating again anyway if there is no more fluid going in. There simply won't be any fluid left to be passed. But here is the caution that comes with the myth of never drinking urine, after the second or third time of recycling your own urine with no other water intake, then the waste products do get too concentrated for the kidneys to handle and that can cause them to shut down, or renal failure, which is fatal.

Fact: Urine drinking has been around for literally thousands of years. It has been considered a medicinal practice for health by nearly every major culture at one point or another through time, since ancient China, India, the Egyptians, Greeks, and Aztecs, in a practice called urotherapy. Even in modern times, there have been bars where people actually pay to drink urine.

Myth: You will *not* die or get sick if you drink urine. It is not poisonous. It is actually sterile the moment it leaves your body, and only contact with the air allows for bacteria to grow. This is why you shouldn't urinate and then store it for later.

- **Alcohol and Cigarettes.** In general it is better to not drink alcohol or smoke cigarettes when you don't have water. It is a medical fact that both of these will only serve to dehydrate you even more. However, if you are craving a cig or a sip, that little reprieve may make you feel better mentally and do much to renew your morale and motivation.

- **Talking Point.** They say talking uses up body fluids and it is true. When water is scarce, try not to speak, and try to breathe through your nose. If you're in the heat of the desert drying up, likely you won't want or be able to talk with your buddy anyway, but it might actually give you an idea that could save your lives.

Humans need hope. When things are tough, a small pleasure can re-instill hope. So, that smoke, booze or chat might be your death knell, but they might also be your salvation.

4

FIRE

Fire is one of the key elements in any survival situation. It provides warmth, light, and heat for cooking. It can sterilize knives for first aid and help you make cooking utensils. It boils water clean. It protects you against predators. You can use it to signal. Obviously, fire is a major necessity in the wild.

Lighters

I hate rubbing sticks together. I don't smoke, but I live with a lighter on my person at all times. If I'm traveling and must pass security without a lighter, I carry a magnifying glass and magnesium bar. First and foremost, always have a lighter on you and another around you! Stash them everywhere you spend time.

There are different types of lighters. Expensive wind-proof kinds are good if you spend time up on mountains or in generally open areas, but the jet-propulsion of their flame can blow out your fledgling fire. Typically, you should seek out a sheltered area to start your fire, so you don't need the wind-proof kind for survival.

Disposable lighters are great, cheap, tiny and easy to come by. Even after the fuel runs out, you can get a spark out of them, which is still good for getting a fire going in a pinch.

Sometimes, you need a lighter for actual "light." In these cases, Zippo types really earn their keep. They can be lit and set down and used as a lamp, a mini stove or just a little fireplace. They can be comfort as a little fire, a little light, a little heat, and that makes a difference. You can also refill them when away from civilization using alternative fuels.

- **Caution:** Some fuels are dangerous.
  Tip: A crucial good habit is to test all gear in your survival kit regularly.
  Tip: *Always carry* a lighter. Everything else that follows is for when you don't.

The Fire Hierarchy

The best way to start a fire is the easiest way. That's why I constantly stress: **always carry a lighter.** Here is a quick overview of the easiest ways to start a fire, in descending order of ease.

- **Primary:** Lighter or matches—always carry them.
- **Alternatives:** Magnesium bars, magnifying glass, chemicals, fuels, electricity, etc.
- **Primitive: Friction:** Rubbing sticks when all else fails, most common and easiest way
  Percussion: Striking steel & stone to create sparks, maybe the most ancient way
  Combustion: Fire-piston compression (too difficult for most survival needs)
  a) Bow Drill—Most friction, least energy, most time to make, needs cordage
  b) Fire Plow—Least prep and skill, most work, no cordage, uses fat sticks

c) Hand Drill—Easier than plow, more skill than bow, no cordage, uses thin sticks

HOW TO MAKE FIRE

The million reasons you should carry a lighter is the number of strokes you will need to get a fire going by rubbing sticks together!

It is hard work, even after you perfect your technique when you have to start from scratch and work with unfamiliar woods and during inclement weather and a bad situation. It is time consuming and can take a toll on you physically and mentally. If you know and accept this, you'll be able to handle the frustration and not quit until you succeed.

Never give up!

Hard Wood vs. Soft Wood

Most survival books state that for starting fires, you use a hard wood against a soft wood. But I have found, when it comes to rubbing sticks together to make fire, is that **two soft woods work best.**

Try the "nail test." If you can stick your thumbnail into a wood and leave a dent, it's a soft wood. If not, it's a hard wood. It's that simple.

Rubbing ANY two dead and dry sticks together long enough and hard enough will get you some friction and some heat. The best place to get the dead dry wood is from the standing trees with dead branches or in bushes with fallen branches hanging on them. Unless you're in a very dry place, you don't want wood off the ground. You don't want something so soft it will crumble.

What I have found to be the very best for fast fire starting is yucca or sotol, hibiscus and other balsa type woods. If you know what they are, let that be your standard. The bamboo saw is a well tested and universally known fire-by-friction starting method. It is also bamboo on bamboo, so no hard against soft wood issues and it's actually a grass!

The real secret here is the friction-to-flame ratio. If the wood is softer, it'll give way quicker to more friction, and the more friction, the quicker the flame comes. But any way you work it, it will be work.

Preparation

Now let's look at the things you need to consider before attempting to start your fire.

- **Location:** First, choose your location wisely.

Here are the key factors regarding location:
Find a spot away from wind, rain, other elements, and harm's way (e.g. under snow-covered tree branches).
Give yourself enough area to work around the fire—cooking, sleeping, drying clothes, etc.
Pick a generally dry spot, and clear away combustible materials from the surrounding ground surface.
Lay some sticks, logs, leaves, rocks, etc. on the ground so your fire is elevated to allow a slight amount of air/oxygen under it, as well as to keep it off the moist ground, which tends to zap a fledgling fire.
Look for soil, rocks, logs, snow, etc. to create a wall around your fire area.

Starter Materials

Once you've found an ideal location, begin to gather up a good supply of starter materials—tinder, kindling, and fuel.

Tinder is the smallest material, and includes all the little fragile things you can find and grind into a powder—think furry, fuzzy, light, and fluffy material.

Kindling is anything slightly larger than tinder, and includes small branches and twigs not much bigger than a match or birthday candle.

Fuel refers to everything larger that will combust and grow into your full-on fire. You should collect fuel of various sizes, starting with 3-to-6 stacks of wood branches that are just bigger than a twig, and then work your way up to a large pile of wrist- or ankle-sized logs.

Fine Strips of Bark

- **Tinder** After getting the initial ember from friction, combustion, heat, or another energy source, tinder is what makes the bridge from spark to flame.

  The basic idea is to get the driest, fluffiest little poof ball you can from whatever is around you for your tinder. Pocket lint, a lock of hair, toilet paper, leaves, and bark can be used to make a **tinder ball**. You can take strips of bark and dried leaves, mix it with whatever other manmade

Pine Needles

materials you can supplement with, and then rub them together and mix them up in your hand and try to make a nice little fluffy ball. Take all the powder and scraps that might have dropped and sprinkle them back into the mix. Once you have a nice wad of fibrous material, spread it a

Bird's Nest

little so as to make a little ball. Then make a dent in that ball and form it into a nest. Then take all the loose powder and shavings and droppings from your friction formation and sprinkle it back into the middle of your nest. You now have a new home for your baby coal, a chariot to transport the coal to its new tepee home.

Another way to get tinder is to look for the tinder fungus. Scan around trees; there is sometimes a black-looking mucky wad that looks like sap has oozed out of a tree and turned dark. But if you look closer, it's actually a fungus growing in some damaged area of tree bark. If you break it off and it's red-brown inside, it's tinder fungus and makes a great way to start a fire.

There is a false tinder fungus, as well, so be wary. This one looks like a clam on the side of the tree. It is striped and grayish looking. Not as good as the true tinder fungus, but in a pinch, it will do. You may use punk wood, the dry rotted dead wood from fallen trees.

In dry environments, dung that is so dry that it's pure powdery white can be crushed up, and the dust helps to get a fire started.

In many areas, you can scrape the loose bark off trees and rub it together into a small pile of dust and flakes that will catch a spark easily.

If everything is wet, look for the slanted trees and take the bark on the underside, peel it off, and underneath the outermost layers you'll find dry bark that you can shave off and crush into a fine tinder.

Pine resin makes a good food and glue, but it also burns very well. This fuel source is called "lighter knot" or "fat lighter." Often a fallen pine tree will have a lot of dried resin that will have oozed and concentrated in the stump, or you can scrape bits oozing off the tree where branches have broken off. Dried pine resin is usually orange or yellowish. This stuff will burn even in rain.

Another great tinder are plants like cattails. Scrape the brown heads to get lots of fluff, and this stuff catches pretty easily. Even if the cattail has been in the rain, the fluffy stuff inside is still dry. Milkweed, if you bust open a dry pod, you'll find lots of hairs that are good tinder. If you don't know one plant from another, try manipulating some to see what's inside. Moss like old man's beard is also good tinder.

Small Twigs

- **Kindling** are the transition linking logs from twigs to sticks. Kindling is to baby food what tinder is to mother's milk. Kindling materials should always start from toothpick size, then up to pencil size, then finger size, then wrist size, then ankle sized.

Everything above that in size is just a big fat log, also known as fuel. The most basic rule: use dry stuff.

Large Sticks and Logs

- **Fuel** If it burns strong, it's fuel. Except in extreme cold, there is little need to make a huge fire. Big fires tend to burn boots, bags, shelters and a lot of firewood. Plan your fuel supplies out to gather enough to see you through the night. Think red man fire: real small and sit real close; **not** white man fire: real big and sit far back.

There might be times when you want a huge fire to signal for help or to make a lot of coals for cooking or a coal bed to sleep warm through the night. Mostly, go easy, as gathering materials itself can be hard work that depletes energy.

The Tepee Method

The "tepee method" is the best and simplest way to prepare your tinder, kindling, and fuel to start your fire. Start by using a bunch of kindling to make a small "tepee" shape—about 1-2 feet tall—that rests on a bed of sticks and tinder. Leave an opening in the tepee for access to the empty space inside. Then take your soft tinder nest and place it right next to that opening.

Once you've generated your tiny coal ember, transport that ember on a small piece of bark or leaf onto the tinder nest (which should be very close by). With the coal atop the tinder nest, begin to gently breathe air onto it, bringing it from a smoldering coal to a beautiful ember and into a fantastic little flame!

Then, place the flaming nest through the opening in the tepee and onto the bed of tinder inside, and continue to nurture it with gentle breaths as it catches the twigs of the tepee on fire. Once the tepee twigs begin to catch fire, gently lay one piece of kindling after another onto the tepee, slowly reinforcing the walls of it as each layer is consumed by your new hungry offspring of flame. After a few minutes, you'll have

Tepee method

a nice little fire and a giant feeling of warmth inside you.

At this point, stay calm and do not rush the process. I have seen more fires killed at this critical juncture by people who are so excited that they over-stack their fire too quickly and crush it. The end result is no fire and a crushed morale.

Now, let's talk about some of the techniques of fire making, or more pointedly, "ember making." Some are very basic; some are really far out there. But as in everything else regarding survival, there are no hard fast rules other than what you can imagine; there are only principles by which you should be guided.

Other Preparations

Here are a few ways to make sure your fire survives the conditions, and you get the most out of it for your purposes.

■ **Fire Pit** There are a few types of fire pits. The main two I suggest using—besides the simplest form of fire pit—are the Dakota pit and the Cross pit.

The Dakota pit is made by digging two adjacent holes a couple feet apart and connecting them with a tunnel. This is helpful in areas with high winds, or when you have less fuel, or when you don't want to be seen. Start your fire above the hole using methods described above, then move it into one of the holes which should already

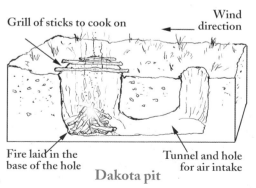

Grill of sticks to cook on

Wind direction

Fire laid in the base of the hole

Tunnel and hole for air intake

Dakota pit

be filled with kindling and fuel. The tunnel and empty connecting hole maintain

Ditches for air intake with fire set at the intersection

Cross pit

air flow to keep the fire going.

The cross pit is just a big "X" dug into the ground so that the wind can still feed your fire while the center of the X lowers the fire so it's not blown all over by the wind.

Most of the time, however, you'll want to make a really simple fire pit. This is done by scraping out a circle of dirt with a stick, rocks, your feet or hands. Make it about six inches deep in the middle and sloping up to ground level on the edges, and about 12-24 inches around. This pit will let more heat get to you at ground level. If you build on flat ground, use rocks to either contain the fire or give you something to cook on. But leave a gap in the rocks facing you to allow heat to reach you directly. If you dig too deep, or make a wall too high, the heat will not be reflected at you but rather straight up.

In all cases, put leaves or logs or twigs down under the fire, as it's better to have the fire start on drier material,

Fire walls

and it allows that little bit of air in there which aids your cause.

■ **Fire Wall** This is a really great supplement to get the most out of your fire. Whether you're sleeping in the open on the ground or in a shelter, it's good to make a wall of some fashion on the opposite side of the fire. This will reflect more heat and light your way and deflect more wind and cold as well. It also keeps the smoke flow down so your face doesn't get smoked out.

Fire walls

You can make a fire wall with sticks and logs, dirt, rocks, a tarp or other manmade materials. The concept is to fashion a wall about a foot behind the fire, extending a couple feet to either side of the fire, and one to three feet high. Make sure it's as wind-proof as you can make it, often by packing the holes with dirt. The specifics of what you build will be dictated by time, terrain, and need.

- **Fire Bed** If you've managed to get a good fire going, but it's freezing and you ain't got a sleeping bag or a very good shelter, then you need yourself a fire bed. Make a big fire by day so you get lots of coals. Dig out an area about the size of your body, but only about six inches deep. When you're ready to sleep, spread your coals evenly inside the hole, and cover them with about three inches of dirt. Depending on the

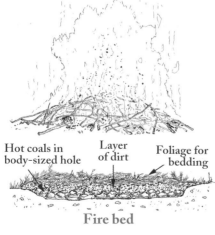

Hot coals in body-sized hole   Layer of dirt   Foliage for bedding

Fire bed

amount of coal and size of the coals, you might need a bit more or less dirt between you and the coals.

Again, this is a supplement for the very cold environment. It takes a lot of work and you might be better off just making a better shelter or sleeping close to your fire and keeping it going throughout the night.

Fire-Starting

First, let's look at some of the better types of wood for primitive fire starting.

Try and find some of these around you or learn to identify the kinds that are available in the area where you intend to travel for work or leisure.

These are everywhere but in general they are found by regions or in specific terrains. To help narrow your focus look for these in your area of interest:

(Some hardwoods included for those keen on still using them.)

Deserts: yucca, sagebrush, mesquite, cottonwood, arrow weed

Arctic: pine

Tropics: bamboo

Jungle: hibiscus, balsa

Seashore: driftwoods

Arid & Mountainous: cedar, thistle stalks

Swamps: cypress

Mountains & Forests: oak, ash, beech, dogwood, elderberry, aspen, poplar, dogbane

Rivers: willows

Deltas & Grasslands: shaving brush tree

Fields: sunflower stalks, mullen stalks

Techniques

Once you've made all preparations including choosing a wise location, gathering your materials, and building a fire wall, it's time to start rubbing sticks! There are many variations on how to start fire with sticks. Each one requires a lot of hard work, many require special accessories, and most require a refined technique. But these are all variables. **Fuel**, **Air**, and **Heat** are the constants. Think: **FAHre**.

You can have gas, wood, paper, or anything that burns as a fuel. You got to have air, not too much to blow it out, especially at the delicate starting stages, but enough for the fuel to combust. And finally, you'll need heat. This might be the spark from a lighter or battery. It might be from a lens of a glass, or it might be from heat generated by friction. In most cases, when you're caught in the wilderness with no tools or resources, it comes down to the friction of rubbing sticks together.

Besides the tried-and-true methods, it is useful to consider a few of the more fascinating techniques of how this universal problem has been solved by other primitive cultures around the world for countless centuries, in that they might assist a beginner.

Fire Plow

The fire plow is the best way to start a fire when you have nothing. It's also the worst way, in that it requires the most work. In a true survival situation—when you have no tools whatsoever—then grabbing two sticks from your environment and using the fire plow technique is the way to make it happen.

The fire plow works best when you have thick sticks of

wood to use. It requires one "plow stick" about the thickness of a broom handle and about a foot long. You also need a "base board," which should be about 2- to 3- feet long and about 2 inches thick. You might use a rock or other object to scrape a running rut or groove into the top face of the base board through which the plow stick will be rubbed back and forth. The technique is not complicated, but it is hard work and hard to master.

First, find a comfortable kneeling position that allows you to hold the base steady either on the ground, in your lap, or wedged into your waist or tummy and the ground at an angle. Then hold your plow stick with both hands, begin rubbing it quickly back and forth into the rut of the base log and begin to develop some friction. I find that keeping the base flat with my foot helps a lot once I have a good groove made. The concept and goal is to rub the plow stick quickly, with force, and with high friction into the base log until it produces heated shavings of powder that eventually become ignited and a coal is generated. Then use that coal to light your gathered tinder by tipping it into your nest.

Fire plow

It's important to find the right angle of pushing down. If your plow stick is pointed too sharply down, you risk digging a hole through your base board. If your plow stick's angle is too close to parallel with the base log, the area of friction is too dispersed and there's no chance for a coal to develop. So, the essential element is to get the right angle to develop friction, then heat, then smoke, then a coal on the end of your plow stick's runway. Be prepared: this takes time.

If your sticks build up too much slickness or get shiny, then there's less friction, so sprinkle a little sand or dry dirt in the base log's groove to roughen it up, or scrape it with something like a rock and get the friction increased. It is hard work, I can't say that enough. It'll make you sweat, make you tired and winded, and even get your muscles fatigued. It just might take hours or days, but you'll eventually get the hang of it, so never quit. And even if you rub and rub for hours without getting fire, you'll be breaking in your base log and plow stick to the process, and when you pick them up to try again later they'll be more apt to get you a coal. Once used successfully, it's easier to do again later.

Once you know how to do this, and have refined your technique as well as developed your sense of which types of wood work best, this can be done in 15-30 minutes given good environmental factors. And once you have your materials broken in, they can often get you a fire in only about five minutes. Of course, if you're completely new to this and in a survival situation for the first time, it could take you an hour or a day of constant work to get a coal.

Hand Drill

Another one of the primitive friction methods for when you have nothing is the hand drill. This is basically the same thing as the fire plow, but the difference is that your friction is pinpointed onto a particular spot on the base, as opposed to a long groove, and the friction is created by quickly spinning the stick on that point instead of rubbing

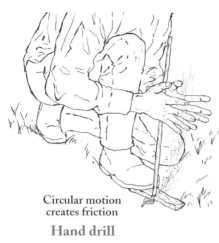

Circular motion creates friction

Hand drill

it lengthwise.

You'll need to make a notch in your wood base, and I find this no easy task without a knife. Not to mention, unless you happen to find some really nice, smooth, thin sticks, without a knife to whittle it down and make it smooth, this technique is not suitable as it requires some modifications to the base and spindle that simply can't be done without an implement of some sort. If you can improvise a knife with a sharp rock or other found object, that will help you create a good enough notch in the base that will focus the friction, and also to smooth out the spindle stick to make it easier to work with.

If you can't make a notch, but have some cordage, tie 2 thin sticks together and drill in the middle groove between them and this will accomplish the same effect as the notch.

Often naturally long spindles occur in the environment that make excellent hand drill spindles because they are long, thin, dry, solid and smooth. Look for reeds that aren't hollow and other similar dry light wooded materials as they give the best chances.

Find or make a good piece of base wood that's flat on top, and make a little notch near the edge of the flat surface that creates an inverted "V" down like a small hole that you can lay some tinder directly under. Best to use a leaf or bark as a catch to hold this tinder so that once the coal is generated, you can transport it to the nest, unlike the plow, which you can just tip into the nest.

Then place your long spindle into the notch and sit down comfortably. Press your hands together with the top of the spindle between them, and rub them together briskly as if you're warming them up. At the same time, apply pressure downwards to create friction and heat. Your palms will slip down toward the base pretty quickly, so when they get to the bottom, hang onto your stick with one hand while holding pressure downward, quickly bring the other hand to the top of the spindle and keep pushing downward, and then bring the bottom hand up and resume the motion. Keep the spindle spinning back and forth and driving down the whole time to keep up friction. If your spindle is not smooth, this activity will not feel good on your hands and will tear them up something fierce. So take the time to smooth out your spindle before starting.

If you have some string, you can dramatically enhance you efforts by making a notch in the top of your stick like those on the back of an arrow shaft. Then take a 6-12 inch string and tie two loops in it for your thumbs. Lay this enhancer string through the slit type notch and insert your thumbs through the loops. This allows you to maintain downward pressure without losing momentum each time you would otherwise have to bring your hands back up the shaft. The end result is more friction, less effort, faster fire. If you don't have the strength to do the fire plow method, this works well.

Fire Bow Drill

If you have a knife and string, then the bow drill method is far better on your back and hands and muscles than most of the other methods.

Materials Needed:

Bow drill

One flat base board (think of a wooden cutting board) that's about an inch or so thick and made of dry, sturdy wood.

One spindle stick, also about an inch thick and straight, that you will use to spin rapidly to create friction. This should be dry, sturdy wood about 12 inches in length.

One wooden block or spindle handle to press down on top of the spindle. This should be a couple inches thick and wide, and should fit into your closed hand, though it can vary; just understand that the purpose of this block is to protect your hand when you're pressing down on the spindle. Strong sea shells, big bone joints or concave rocks work well and think about using some grease, fat, or other substance to lube the handle to reduce friction and heat as well as increase spin for the base and coal.

One bow. This should be about an inch thick, two feet long, green/fresh wood so that it's strong yet flexible, and not brittle or easily breakable. It needs to be strong and thick enough to take your weight as you put downward pressure on the spindle.

One long, sturdy string (when necessary, even a 6-inch piece will do).

First, carve a round indentation with your blade tip on the top face of your baseboard, less than an inch from either long end.

Then cut a "V" notch on the underside edge of the base board directly perpendicular to the indent. When you're ready to start the fire, place the board on something like a sheet of bark or leaves to catch and hold the dust that results; it's that dust with your bit of tinder that will catch and give you a coal.

Next, carve the fire-making tip of your spindle to a bluntly rounded point in order to fit into the indenture of the baseboard. Cut the top of the spindle into more of a point in order to reduce overall friction in the spindle handle.

Prepare the wooden block of the spindle handle by carving a shallow round groove in its face into which the top of the spindle can be held in place as you press down on it. This is where a hard wood really comes in handy.

For the bow, use whatever string you have—almost any thickness will do, but a sturdy boot string will usually do the trick if it's thick and not made of synthetics, as they have a tendency to melt under a lot of friction. It's also best to use something else if you don't want to risk losing your boot lace, but it'll have to do when you don't have anything else. Obviously, the amount of string or cordage you have will be the best determinant for the size of your bow. These can work with even a six-inch piece of string, so don't despair.

Cut notches on both ends of your bow about an inch from the ends, and tie either end of the string into these notches, making sure that the tautness of the string creates a bowing effect on the spindle handle (just think of a toy bow and arrow set you had as a kid).

Sit or kneel next to your prepared tepee and tinder nest, lay the base down, and put the shavings and other tinder directly under the "V" notch on the base. With the string taut and in place on the bow, loop it once around the middle of the spindle, positioning the spindle at the middle of the string. Then place the blunt point of the spindle into the base indent, and position the block on the top of the spindle. Now you're ready to begin.

The basic motion you need to employ is like using a saw. Hold the bow with one hand and press down on the block with the other keeping the spindle in place in the base indent, then begin "sawing" the bow back and forth. As you do this, the string will cause the spindle-point to rotate quickly in the notch, creating friction. Once you get a good rhythm going, you will begin to generate significant friction, then heat, then a coal or ember that will light your tinder.

If you prepare all your tools properly, this is one of the easiest ways to start a fire for beginners. It can vary in size and shape, but basically speaking, mechanics and physics do the work for you.

Fire Piston

This technique is pretty easy once it is refined. It is a combustion method based on a piston-style pump. The materials required include one hollow tube such as bamboo, one piston/stick that fits snugly inside the tube, and tinder.

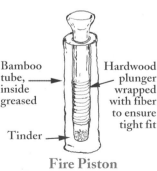

Bamboo tube, inside greased

Hardwood plunger wrapped with fiber to ensure tight fit

Tinder

Fire Piston

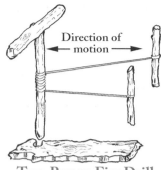

Two-Person Fire Drill

The theory is that by pushing downward on the piston into the tube, high pressure is created which generates heat very quickly and ignites the tinder at the bottom of the tube.

This is sometimes made by fitting one piece of naturally-hollow bamboo tightly into another, or by hollowing out a piece of wood and then finding another stick that fits perfectly into that hollowed out space. You can also use a small piece of string or leather to create a seal and hold the tinder in place. Usually some lubricant such as a fat or oil is used lightly to enhance the seal and increase the performance of the pump itself.

This method makes it easy to get a coal, which is the real hard part of all the other friction methods for fire starting. However, it may also be the hardest technique to make from materials, in terms of the details necessary to get the precision seal.

Bamboo Fire Saw

Take one segment of bamboo, the driest piece

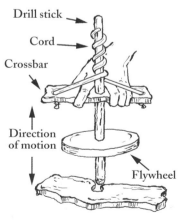

Pump Fire Drill

you can get, and cut it in half lengthwise. Take one piece and make a notch in the middle of the outside wall, perpendicular to its length. On the inside of that piece, make a lengthwise notch and load some tinder into it. If you have a knife, scrape the outside of the bamboo to make shavings, which makes fantastic tinder.

To hold tinder in place, use a twig laid lightly over it. Hold it in place with your thumbs.

Take the other bamboo half and place one end on the ground at an angle, and secure the other end tucked into your stomach or wedged into your lap. Sharpen one edge a bit. Then take the notched bamboo piece and fit the outside notch into the edge of the bottom bamboo—the insides of that bamboo piece and the tinder bundle will be up facing you. Gather your tinder around the inside of the notch and start sawing back and forth along the edge of the grounded bamboo. Make sure you keep the tinder in place near the notch that's guiding the sawing motion.

Keep sawing like this until the friction and heat ignite your tinder well enough for you to stop and transport it. Do not stop as soon as there is smoke; keep going until you can see the ember. You can invert these if you need more downward pressure.

- **Alternative Fire Saw.** If there's no bamboo available, you can try this technique with other sticks or small logs.

Find a 3-foot solid "base" log and carve an edge on it as sharp as you can—this will be the piece that you wedge between the ground and your lap or stomach.

Then take another piece of wood that's long enough to hold in either hand while you slide it back and forth across the edge of the base log. Make a small hole in the center of this piece, and pack that space with some tinder, tightly

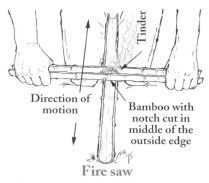

Direction of
motion

Tinder

Bamboo with
notch cut in
middle of the
outside edge

Fire saw

enough to stay in place but loosely enough to allow some air in for ignition. On the other side of the hole, make a notch that will run along the edge of the base log. Then begin sawing just like with the bamboo saw. This will create heat and ignite the tinder.

When It Is Wet

Getting a fire going in wet conditions is challenging but it can be done. Look for dry stuff around trees that have a slight tilt, or if the rain is coming down at an angle—look for the dry parts of trees where they're not exposed to the rain. Look for the branches and leaves in these dry areas and scrape some bark off that dry part of the tree.

You can find dry wood inside the bark: pick up a few branches and peel off the wet outer bark. Look under piles of leaves. Look for dry nooks and crannies and little spaces that might have avoided wetness. If you find dry items, and they are not the right size, shave them down into kindling and tinder.

Prepare your place for your protected fire and make it as dry as possible. You'll need enough area around you to stay dry, dry your clothes, store and dry firewood, cook, work and rest. Survival is like chess, you must think as many moves ahead as you can.

When It Is Cold

Another harsh environment is the Arctic. If you're without anything else, try using ice to start a fire.

It has to be a very sunny day. Take a chunk of ice and do your best to form it into a sort of magnifying glass lens. Then, with all the other principles of preparation, supplies, and patience, you can attempt to use the ice as a magnifying glass to light a tinder bundle and make a fire (see magnifying glass technique below).

Alternative Fire Starters and Helpers

■ **Magnifying Glass.** Let's start with the best option besides the lighter, and that's the magnifying glass. This is a great piece of kit, and I always carry one. It's really an eternal source of fire so long as you have sunlight. The bigger the glass, the easier to start a fire and the better chance you have when the sun isn't as bright.

The technique is simple. Get into a comfortable position in which you can sit a while. Hold the magnifying glass a few inches above the tinder, and maneuver it so that the sunlight is focused through it and pinpointed directly into the middle of your tinder. When you begin to see wisps of smoke, begin to gently blow or fan the tinder until a flame or ember appears. Then transfer the ember as described above.

Note that you don't need an actual magnifying glass, though they do work the best. Practical substitutes include flashlight lens, glass bottle, any convex shard of glass, and so on.

Another trick when using a magnifying glass is the

cigarette technique. Now I don't smoke, but I always carry a lighter. And when I go to the field I often carry a pack of cigarettes both to trade with local tribes and as a good primitive method for treating parasites (more on that later). The main thing here is that it's much easier to get a fire going with a cigarette than with an ember or coal, and it can be easier to light a cigarette with a magnifying glass than it is to ignite tinder.

- **Hand Cleaner.** Commercially available "hand sanitizers" are very good for starting fires. A bit of hand cleaner added to the tinder ignites and stays lit.

- **Vaseline.** Many soldiers carry Vaseline gauze dressings in their first aid kit. They're super for starting a fire as the petroleum jelly-covered gauze catches easily. Campers and outdoorsman for years have used cotton balls soaked in Vaseline as a reliable fire starter.

- **Perfume.** Depending on your situation, check in your inventory of supplies and see if anyone has any perfume, aftershave, or other astringents. Now, if the first ingredient in the product is water, it likely won't work. But if the main ingredient is ETOH or alcohol, you have a good fire-starting enhancement.

- **Booze.** Some of the higher-proof drinking alcohols will also help start a fire.

- **Batteries.** If you have batteries with enough juice left in them, and two little wires, or any pieces of metal to conduct, it's easy to start a fire. Just connect one wire each to the positive and negative on the battery. Then touch them together on top of your tinder to make a spark and get an ember. You can use this spark with some fuels. If there is not enough to make spark, but the wires touching each other creates heat, keep them ground on each other and lay them on some tinder or lay some tinder on them and wait for them to heat up enough to ignite it that way. If using a gadget like a flashlight or toy, connect the wires, turn it on and add it to the tinder to heat up to the point of ignition.

- **Steel Wool.** Note that some forms of steel wool work better than others. Simply touch it to your batteries, it heats up, ignites and can then be used to start your fire.

- **Char-Cloth.** It is created when cloth is essentially cooked without being burned. Place some good cloth in a can or wrapped in some metal and leave in the fire until black. This material catches a spark easily to help make fire when you can't find good tinder.

- **Pine Sap.** It's great to use in helping to get a flame. Always look for it.

- **Flint and Other Rocks.** These take a little practice at finding and identifying. If you happen to have rocks lying around, time on your hands, and need for a fire, just start grabbing rocks and striking them against one another to see if you get sparks. If you do, that's all you need to know.

    If you have a piece of steel or a knife, this is preferable, but flint and another rock can work as many rocks have some sort of iron or pyrite metal ore which acts like steel creating a spark when struck against flint. Even with a nice piece of flint and a good strong steel knife blade, it takes a little practice to get the strike angle right for creating sparks. This is the principle for modern lighters—flint and steel make a spark, which ignites the gas, which results in a flame. Flint is found all over, but more so in some places than others. It's grey, brown, or black and if you break it, it will look like a clam shell sort of pattern.

- **Rubber.** Rubber is a great fire enhancer. Many survivalists cut up small pieces from an old inner tube and throw these into their survival kits. Rubber never rusts or decays, and it can even get wet and still burn. It won't catch a spark, but rubber will help a tiny fire get big in a hurry! So look for any rubber from wreckage, it will serve you well for fire making especially in inclement weather.

- **Any Fuel, Oil, Fat, Grease or Lubricants.** Take a good creative look. Even cooking oil or sun tan oil might come in handy for making a fire, or keeping one going in foul weather.

- **Stuffing from Car Seats, etc.** Another potential source for fire starting that is often overlooked. Be willing to rip up a nice car seat to get that stuffing, or break apart some structure to get at some part of it that might be useful.

- **Termite Nests.** These can be used for building fires, and note that they make a lot of smoke. I've heard everything about termite-nest smoke, from curing foot fungus to scaring off jaguars to diminishing mosquitoes. And you can eat termites, too—a 2-for-1 special.

- **Dry Powdery Plants.** Some plants lend themselves well to specific needs of man. The puffball mushroom is a great example. They aren't everywhere, but if they're around, you'll know them as they're an oddly round-shaped mushroom that if you give a little kick, it will turn into powder—great for fire starting. So look at all the plants around you and experiment with everything you find. You never know; and you might have the rest of your life to find out. Pine cones, cattail, dandelions (when in spore) and many mosses are good for fire starters.

- **Processed Foods.** Some foods like Cheetos™ and Pringles™ are known to burn well as fire starters, due to their high fat content and being processed. Most processed foods have a layered structure that permits air to let them burn well.

- **Tampons.** If these are available, they're great as tinder—be sure to fluff it up first.

- **First Aid Dressings.** These are also great for starting fires as they are perfectly dry and light so they take a spark readily.

- **Condoms.** These are not for fire starting directly, but condoms are fantastic for keeping things dry and/or carrying them with you to stay dry for later usage.

- **Fire from Trash.** The same principle of the magnifying glass or the flash light reflector can basically be applied to anything highly shiny and bendable enough to focus the sun's light. I've heard of everything from a dark chocolate candy bar to toothpaste being used to scour and polish the bottom of an aluminum can.

- **Magnesium Bar.** This is a good piece of kit to have with you whenever traveling. It works in any climate, even wet, and is simple to operate. Strike the flint to send sparks into the magnesium bar shavings which ignite and light your tinder.

- **Candles.** Store-bought and improvised candles won't necessarily help you get a fire started, but they're very handy to have as they keep a flame with little effort or oversight—as long as you keep them protected from the elements.

Travel With Fire

This is an important part of survival. As getting a fire is difficult enough, if you can't repeat the process or find another way but need to travel, then transporting your fire is crucial.

Punk wood, or dry rotted wood that is not wet is good for carrying a coal at a smolder.

Tinder fungus will do the same, but must be tended during travel to keep the ember.

Packing packets, such as dried grass made into a bundle with the coal placed in the middle and then wrapped with bark to protect and tied with cordage to keep sealed, work well.

In all cases, care must be taken to ensure not too much air gets in or it will catch fire, but not enough air will suffocate and snuff your coal.

Torches can be made from many things. Take branches, reeds or just strips of dried bark, beat them with a stick to soften and then bundle them together tightly. Dip in a fuel if you have it, otherwise, plain will work. The longer the torch, the longer it lasts.

Making Cooking Utensils

Along with fire-making comes another very important, but often overlooked, aspect of fire use in survival—what to cook in. If you have pots and pans, or metal cups or tin cans, you're sorted. When you're truly surviving with nothing, these simple things are often the most difficult problems to solve.

- **Bamboo for Cooking.** Not only can you use bamboo to start a fire, as a food source, as a water source, as material

Bamboo pot
for cooking food

for making shelter and more, you can cook in it too. Start by cutting out one enclosed segment of bamboo. Then cut a hole into the side of the segment large enough to get your food into, or simply cut one end off the segment to create an enclosed tube.

To cook in this vessel, place it with the food/liquid near the fire, but not actually in or on it, and leave it there until the bamboo blackens and hardens (called "curing"). After it's cured, you can put it closer or even above the fire, but keep an eye on it in case it actually catches fire. I have boiled water for a full 30 minutes using a bamboo vessel, and have used the same cured "pot" for a long time.

Bamboo pot
for heating water

- **Coconuts.** Coconut shells are the best natural thing I've found and used for boiling and cooking in. I've placed them right in the fire and watched them transfer the heat and boil the water and not burn. It's safest to place them on the side of the fire instead of on or above it, but they are fairly resistant to catching fire.

- **Turtle Shell.** I have seen turtle shells used by tribal locals for cooking, and so I know they work. I myself have cooked turtles in their own shells, and that works swell!

- **Conch Shells.** Their capacity isn't great but a half dozen of them placed around your fire can sterilize the water quantities needed and cook a little food.

- **Carved-Out Wood.** Given enough free time and lack of other materials, get a nice piece of hard wood, then cut, shave, or otherwise manipulate it to become a pot. Then try to spot-burn the center by concentrating fire on its middle while keeping the outsides free from flames. Once the middle is sufficiently burnt out, use a rock or stick to start hollowing out the middle. Do cycles of burn-carve, burn-carve until you reach your goal.

Bowl is formed by burning then carving with a rock

Wooden Bowl

- **Birch Bark.** This bark is great for many survival needs. Birch has a flexible and hardy paper-like bark that allows you to form it and place it filled with water near a fire without burning; it will transfer heat and boil water. Make a box or a cone, with wood pegs to hold them fastened, then prop it next to fire to boil water.

General cooking concepts

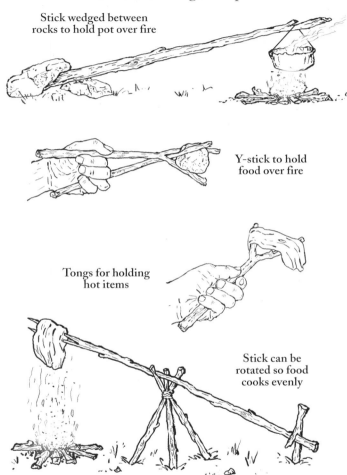

Stick wedged between rocks to hold pot over fire

Y-stick to hold food over fire

Tongs for holding hot items

Stick can be rotated so food cooks evenly

5

FOOD

We need food to live, but in a survival situation, food won't be a top priority. Once all the greater needs are sorted out, then start thinking about gettin' some groceries.

Now when you got it, save it first!

Rationing

Rationing is simple math. Take the amount of food you have, divided by how many people there are, divided by how many days you expect to be in survival mode.

Amount ÷ Number of People ÷ Duration

Time is the one thing that you'll have no control over. For this "infinite" potential, you'll need to assign a number based on the law of averages. This is your variable.

Caloric Intake and Output

Calorie Facts for Average Humans:
Men need about 2,500 calories per day.
Women need about 2,000 calories per day.
Children and the elderly need a bit less.
Large people and fit people need a bit more.

We only burn about 20% of daily calories through activity and exercise.
70% of these calories are actually spent on all the organs working all day.
10% are burned off while processing the food from which you're getting the calories.
Studies vary, but most folks will expend about 1,800 calories just sitting there for a day.

Calories from Food in the Wild:

One pound of fat is worth about 3,500 calories.
Wild meats tend to be about 500 calories per pound (rabbit, deer, boar, etc.).
Fish are around 750 calories per pound on average (the range is wide).
Shellfish and seafood are around 350 calories per pound.
Vegetables come in way low at around 100-200 calories per pound (the range is wide; roots and tubers provide more calories than other veggies).
Fruits are about double the veggie value at 300-400 calories/pound.
Milk has about 2,500 calories per gallon (if you can find a wild goat or other source).
Eggs offer about 100 calories per egg.
Nuts are great for pure survival energy, with 2,500 calories per pound.
Beans are an awesome energy food with about 1,250 calories per pound.

Now that you have an idea what humans burn in a day and what general foods provide in terms of energy-resource value, you can better figure out how to ration.

Use general rules as a guide then chuck it right out the window and prove it wrong.

Humans Will Likely Die If They Go More Than:
3 minutes without air
3 hours of extreme exposure (heat or cold, desert, arctic, freezing water)
3 days without water
3 weeks without food

If your will is strong, I say you can prove all these limits wrong. They are, however, good and standard guidelines for planning and assessing any situation.

Now, let's say it all goes horribly wrong. What does that look like?

Phases of Starvation

Determined humans can go 8-12 weeks without food, provided they have adequate water and a strong will to live. So, you have at least two months, if you're drinking water. Humans can lose around 50% of their total weight and then make a full recovery.

- **Hungry and Mad—Week 1** The first phase is hunger. Irritability and lethargy or tiredness may result from lack of food and lower blood-sugar levels.

  Key: This is the anger phase, when people are very grumpy and irritable.

- **Very Hungry and Sad—Week 2** The second phase of starvation is obvious loss of weight, and diminishing muscle mass. During this phase, most people no longer experience normal hunger, and sex drive decreases markedly.

Key: This is when people begin to suffer serious bouts of depression and self doubt.

- **Starving and Crazy—Week 3** This phase could have swelling and decreased ability of the body to digest. Organs start shrinking and losing some function during this stage.

  Key: This is when people start acting crazy and extreme; they begin getting desperate.

- **Starved and Subdued—Week 4** At this point of starvation, people experience neurologic malfunctions including hallucinations, convulsions, and severe muscle pains, as well as irregular heartbeat and shallow breathing.

  Key: There is no extra energy for fighting or even crying, it is a hanging-on phase.

  The best medicine is a slow but constant pace of working towards some practical goal. **Stick together** if in a group or **keep it together** if alone.

Ethics and Honor in Survival

Doing the right thing in bad times. My SF brethren have a saying that Green Berets are Uncle Sam's extremists. We hold fast the philosophy, "Who believes longest and strongest will always win," and we believe! I also like to put it another way "SF is where the bad boys get to be the good guys!" That summarizes the difference between SF and other troops. We must have that "built-in" morale compass that guides us through.

I don't teach all of the S.E.R.E. (Survival, Escape, Resistance & Evasion) training methods of the Green Berets because a lot of it simply isn't applicable to a civilian survivor.

But there are two tenets at the core of the S.E.R.E. course you should know:

First: Plan on walking home. Hope for rescue, but plan to get yourself out.

Second: Learn to survive, fight to survive, and live to return—with honor.

Everyone will break at one point or another. The key is to do your best, bounce back afterwards, and at all times, even during the breaking, try to keep your sense of honor.

One last note on attitude and contagion. Fear spreads faster than any virus. If someone is in panic, calm 'em down ASAP. Likewise, bravery and honor is contagious.

- **Cannibalism** Gruesome as it is, it warrants a realistic discussion because it has, does, and will occur, and cannot be ignored just because we find it tasteless.

    First, throw out the option of auto-cannibalism— chopping off your pinky to nibble on for sustenance. The reasons are simple and pragmatic. The loss of blood, the stress and pain, the potential exposure to infection, are against consuming your own body parts, unless you lost the body part in some traumatic accident.

    How might cannibalism apply in a group situation? As long as it doesn't harm anyone, if someone is dead already, why let the dead person's flesh go to waste? The only rule is that you must not kill your own kind to live—that is murder, but cannibalism after death, for life, is not.

KILLING IS LIFE

- **Meat: It does a body good!** Animals and insects can meet about 90% of all your nutrition needs in a survival situation, and it's an easier and safer bet to catch and kill animals than trying to subsist off of plants alone. Ounce for ounce, you will always get the most calories from meat over any other food source out there.

About 90% of bugs and animals can be eaten by humans, but 90% of plants cannot.

Everywhere you go on the planet, there is animal/insect life. Taking these two fundamental principles is why the military teaches primarily to rely on hunting rather than gathering for food.

- **That means killing.** There are many ways to kill, but there is no nice way to kill. All you can do is dispatch it as quickly as you can, be thankful and survive.

For survival hunting, simple is always best. It is usually a two-part process:

1. Disable or hurt it enough so that it stops moving, at least for a moment.

2. Dispatch or kill it the very second you get the chance to finish it off.

Catching Animals

Before you can kill an animal and eat it, you have to catch it. So you need to find it.

Tracking
When you are hungry, start hunting. If the prey is there, you will find tracks or signs.

Once you find these, make two key determinations:
Are the tracks of something too big for you to bother with?
If they are not too big, are they fresh enough to be worth pursuing?

Tracks usually lead to one of three places: **Home**, **Food**, or **Water**. And the finding of any one of these is a good thing. You might find their food source and be able to eat it, or their water source and drink up, or their home and then you eat them.

Feces is usually found around tracks, so the two work together for the beginner survivor. It's the feces that gets the novice tracker's attention to notice the tracks and follow them.

The cats have retractable claws, and dogs don't—so look for the claw marks. Generally, paw pads with claw scrapings means some sort of canine critter, and paw pads without means some kind of feline animal.

Many small game make tracks with or without claws. If the tracks are from hooves, then they're fair game as long as they're not too big. If too big, follow to water or food.

As for droppings, look for freshness and what they've eaten.

Hunting

The Four Basics Hunting Styles, in Order of Effectiveness:
Tracker: You find tracks and hunt down the animal's trail. This provides good chances of success. (Herding animals into a trap or ambush is considered part of this group.)

> **Waiter:** You find a home or watering hole or feeding ground, and wait, hidden. When an animal approaches, wait until it gets near to you and then pounce with your weapon to disable and kill.

> **Baiter:** Set out some bait and hope an animal comes to take the bait. You can set the bait in a trap, or in the open—in which case you would wait and pounce when a critter came for it.

> **Ranger:** Roam around until you encounter and engage. This is not the best technique on its own, but you should always be a "ranger" when on the move or while out doing other tasks like finding water, shelter, etc.

Now let's look at some of the basic considerations of hunting.

- **Time of Day** Start in the morning, at first light or just before. This is when many critters are most active. The night dwellers will be headed for home and the day dwellers will be looking for breakfast.

  Do not hunt at night, do not to risk hunting at dusk: the predators come out at night and can see in the dark. Also, it is very easy to get disoriented in the dark and end up spending a night away from your camp. If you must hunt at dusk, keep a fire lit, keep it in sight, and hunt for the things that might come to check out your fire's light. Big things tend to stay away from fires, smaller, more inquisitive critters often come for a peek.

- **Size** Don't tackle anything bigger than you or that is more than you can use.

  If something spots you, freeze. Just be still and be patient. When it carries on, so do you.

  If it's after you, try to make a slow, cautious withdrawal. Keep eyes on it at all times.

Always carry a near, far, and too-dang-close weapon.

Stay mobile and always work to the outside of any game's striking range. All animals strike from their center, keep moving in circles around them to break their concentration.

- **Scent** Stay downwind, so that your scent doesn't blow to the animals and alert them.

Snares and Traps

Use these techniques for smaller creatures.

The basic principles of traps and snares are like hunting, except hunting is all about mobility operations, and "snaps" (snares and traps) are about static operations. The old real estate axiom comes to mind—location, location, location! Choose your "real estate" carefully. Apply the same techniques for hunting—drops and tracks, then find a home, hole or feed spot—and set up your "snap."

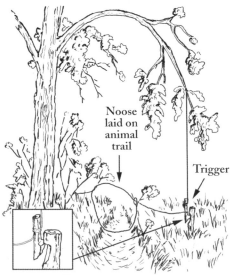

Noose laid on animal trail

Trigger

Snare preparation

Snaps take a lot of time and work to initially set up. After that, they require vigilance to check regularly to either get your catch or re-set your trap or improve it. Be patient, expect failures at first, but it will improve.

There are many different types of snaps but it's better to know one or two snaps well, that work well, that you can make quickly, effectively and place plenty of them.

What is the difference between a trap and a snare? In the simplest terms: string!

- **Snares** If you have cordage of any kind, you can make a simple snare. The cordage provides the mechanism for tension. So, remember it this way: **snare** the **hare**.

Snares are anything that will snatch your prey. The best snare is the basic and simplest one. Easy to make, so you can make several quickly and increase your odds by placing more of them.

The **spring snare** is just what it says on the label. The best way to make a spring snare is to take a small sapling tree and bend it over to look like an upside down "U"; then tie a small piece of string to its top, and tie the other end of that string to a little hook carved from a piece of wood

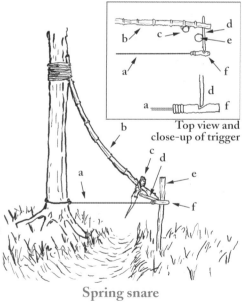

Top view and close-up of trigger

Spring snare

which is then hooked onto a small stake in the ground with a notch to hold it; then tie another piece of string in a circle with a loosely fitted slip knot, and hold it open using two small twiglets.

Choose a sapling that's just on the side of a game trail, and add bait to lure the critter. It puts its head into the loop to get at the bait, and in doing so, it disturbs and inadvertently tugs on the looped string. This causes the string to pull the little wooden hook out of the notched wooden stake, releasing the tension on the little sapling tree which then springs back up to it's original upright position.

In the process, it snatches the noose tight around the critter's neck, snatches its body off the ground, and holds it dangling off the ground with the noose choking the life out of it. It dies, you find it and eat it. (If you don't have bait, place it on a pathway that the creature will need to pass; the same result ensues.)

- **Bait and Place.** Both snares and traps can be used with bait or place techniques. "Bait" involves food or other form of attraction to lure an animal into the snap. "Place" simply means that you situate the snap on a well-used animal trail or lair. Ideally, you'd employ both.

Choose a good location, right outside of the animal's home, hole, lair, etc. Or choose a spot near the feeding grounds or watering hole that looks well used. The principle is that, no matter which route the critter takes, it will always come home, need water, and go to feed.

If you don't find such obvious sites, but you're onto a good game trail, many critters will use a trail like a highway, then use the game trail for your location. When you do this, "**channel or funnel**" the critters into your trap

Front View

Top View

Snare placement

Animal is funneled into the snare from either direction

by laying logs, rocks, sticks and brush in a way so that it funnels them into your trap *both ways*! Picture an hourglass angle from above, so that a "V" focuses them into your trap from either direction of approach.

Important: In all cases of snaps, be sure to reduce the amount of human scent on all of your snap materials.

- **Traps** If you don't have cordage, then you have no capacity for tension to make a snare and must use a different principle of physics to create a trap. Basically, traps use leverage or gravity as the mechanism of tension. The trigger is the loss of balance cause by the animal's movement, allowing gravity to apply the energy to execute your trap. Remember it like this: **slap** the **trap**. Just like you'd slap your hand down to catch a mouse trying to escape, your trap will slap down on your prey.

Figure-4 Deadfall. This is the most basic and common trap. You can use a large rock, heavy log, or other similar object to crush the critter. As an alternative method,

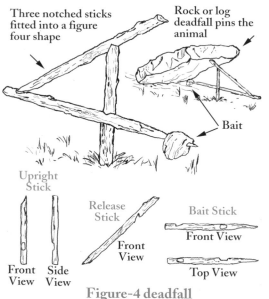

Three notched sticks fitted into a figure four shape

Rock or log deadfall pins the animal

Bait

Upright Stick

Release Stick

Front View

Bait Stick

Front View

Front View

Top View

Front View   Side View

Figure-4 deadfall

instead of a large rock or log, you can build and employ a box, cage, or basket to fall onto the critter and trap it there until you come to finish it off.

The Figure-4 is easy to make, and can be constructed even without a knife by using your fingernails or a sharp rock. Picture the numeral 4. There are three lines in the numeral 4—one vertical, one horizontal, and one angled. Each of these lines will be a stick or log in your Figure-4 Deadfall, they will be held together with notches, and they will all stand under the weight of the deadfall.

While the basic snare and the common Figure-4 Deadfall trap are the easiest and best to use for the novice, here are a few other methods of making traps that you may consider trying.

- **Nets.** If you have a net, you can use the snare method but replace the noose with the net. You can also use nets to catch birds and fish.

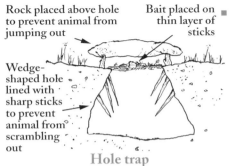

Rock placed above hole to prevent animal from jumping out

Bait placed on thin layer of sticks

Wedge-shaped hole lined with sharp sticks to prevent animal from scrambling out

Hole trap

■ **Holes.** When all else fails, start digging holes. Dig your holes (size and placement) based on the type of animal you hope to catch. Try to loosely cover it with light twigs and leaves, making sure that an animal can break through this cover and that the hole is deep enough to contain them once they do. If you have bait, place some in the middle of the cover above the hole. Consider placing sharp stakes in the hole, one in a cone or a few if flat bottomed.

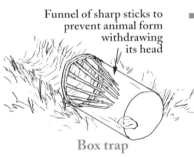

Funnel of sharp sticks to prevent animal form withdrawing its head

Box trap

■ **Boxes.** Another technique is making cages or boxes with a small hole for the critter to stick its head in and inverted spikes to hold the animal's head from pulling out, like a Chinese finger trap. The animal will press its head through the opening to nibble at the bait, but it won't be able to get its head out.

Fishing Techniques

If you're anywhere near water, going fishing is always a smart option. Tackle is not that difficult to make in the wild, the techniques of catching fish are varied and achievable, and almost all fish are good and safe to eat.

- **Lines** are a bit tricky to come by and create, though very doable. Whatever line you use, always make your string and hook can support whatever fish you're after.

Thorn hooks

- **Hooks** are very simple to make. Any safety pin, paperclip, or other piece of bendable metal can be used. Make a good anchor point for tying the string and sharpen the working end as best you can, or make a barb or trap so that once they bite down, they can't get their lip back off the hook.

The key is to fashion your material into the classic "J" shape that marks most hooks, sharpen the point on the hook end,

Safety Pin hook

Pin hooks

and fashion a notch or a barb near that point that will catch on the inside of the fish's mouth once it goes in. You can use the small joints in tree branches which provide a natural angle, and then sharpen the smaller end's point; then make a notch on the anchor point at which to mount the line.

Wood sliver with carved barb

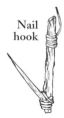

Nail hook

A good simple technique for any hook you make is to create a "barb or gouge." Just imagine a small toothpick with a notch groove around the middle. Tie your string there, put your bait on the whole stick in line with the string. When the fish bites and you pull, the stick

Fishing barb

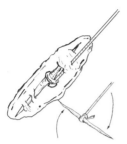

Barb held flat along the
fishing line by the bait . . .

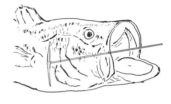

. . . when the bait is swallowed, the
barb opens out perpendicular to
the line and catches in the gullet
of the fish

turns perpendicular to your sting and in effect makes a
barb-gouge in its throat that it can't spit out.

- **Poles** are very helpful if you need to get your hook out
  farther into the water than you can without it. It also helps
  for taking some of the tension off your hand from pulling
  in the fish. If you have to put a lot of line on the pole to
  get it out farther, once you get a fish on the line, place the
  pole on the ground and your foot on the pole and then
  work the fish in by the string.

- **Weights** are sometimes needed either to cast out or to get
  your baited hook down to the bottom.

- **Bait** is anything that you think will make the fish bite the
  hook. Bugs and animal guts are usually the best bait.

- **Lures** are a good substitute for when you don't have bait.
  Anything like feathers or light pieces of cloth can be used
  to mimic a fly or other insect. Anything shiny can be used
  as a "spoon" to get the underwater biters—tops of coke
  cans, small pieces of plastic, metal, or anything shiny that
  you can trim to a small piece and tie off to your string. Tie

it just above your hook so it moves around right in front of but won't stop the fish from getting a bite on your hook.

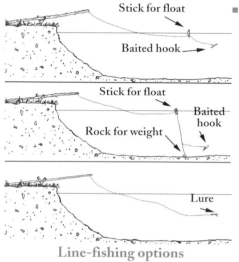

Line-fishing options

- **Floats** are useful in two ways. If you're after mid-depth feeders or just-under-the-surface feeders, then you want to mount to your line a piece of stick or plastic that will float on the water so your eye can see it, but will hold your baited hook suspended underwater and off the bottom, at the depth you set.

The other way to use a float is just to let it get your hook out into the water where you want it. It will still function as a "bobber," but you're also using it to help in your placement by letting it float over to where you want, either with current or wind.

- **Poisons** are also an effective means of catching fish, using naturally occurring roots and/or nuts in the water to disable fish. Acorns are a superb fish poison—mash them up as finely as possible and then dump the material into the water. Any of the roots or nuts that make water milky when applied are likely to be good. You'll need a still area in the water so the current doesn't dilute your poison.

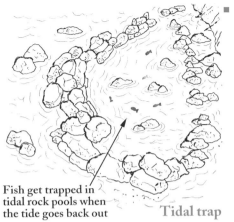

Fish get trapped in
tidal rock pools when
the tide goes back out   **Tidal trap**

■ **Fish traps** are an alternative when you've no strings or hooks. You can make traps for use in the sea, rivers, lakes, or ponds. In the sea, find a natural pool that fills up at high tide and becomes visible at low tide, and then build a gated fence with sticks and/or stones surrounding it. For the sea, when the tide is high, chum your pool to lure fish in and then block the exit when the tide begins to go or the fish you want are trapped.

The best river trap is made by building a "V"-shaped wall of stones and/or sticks that will funnel fish downstream into the open end of the "V" and through a small opening at the point that leads to a holding pen also built with sticks/rocks.

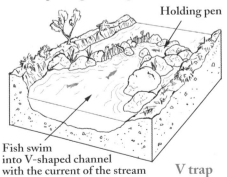

Holding pen

Fish swim
into V-shaped channel
with the current of the stream   **V trap**

For ponds, pick an area where you can make a "V"-shaped fish pen, then chum the pen area and try herding or scaring the fish into your pen. Since there is no current to help keep them in place, have a spear or club ready to disable and kill the fish that appear.

- **Spears** are good but take some skill to master. The points have to be very small and very sharp, and include several points on the end. The best kind are long thin spears with small nails at the end filed very sharp and positioned in a circular pattern, as opposed to horizontal like a dinner fork.

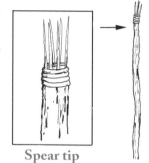
Spear tip

- **Sticks** can be used with some success in shallow waters. Stand in the shallow water and position yourself perfectly still, then wait. If you see fish swimming by and close to the surface, swing hard and directly at the fish's head.

- **Nets** are great tools if you have them. String the net across the stream or river in a manner known as a "gill net," placing it close to the inside bank of a river bend and going as far out into the stream as its length allows. In the

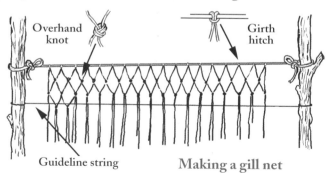
Making a gill net

sea or on a deep lake, if you have a vessel from which to fish, you can fasten weights to the corners of the net to hold it down just below the surface, then pull it up quickly to try to catch anything that may be in it. You can also use a net by standing on the bank of a river or lake and employ it by casting it on top of fish that swim by—just make sure the perimeter of the netting has enough weights tied to it to hold the fish down in the water long enough for you to quickly approach and club.

Net is staked on the bank and into the bed of the stream at both sides

Direction of flow

Positioning a gill net

You can also use the simple scooping-type nets to catch fish. If you have a smaller net or finer mesh, use that for the minnows and eat up. Or use the big net to try and head them off or divert them into the net, and then swing them onto shore or your raft.

- **Light** is an effective tool for hunting lots of things. Laser lights and flashlights that you point and maneuver on the surface can lure freshwater fish as they are attracted to the light and may check it out, allowing you to club or spear the fish. You can also hunt crayfish and frogs and lots of other critters with a flashlight as they are dumbfounded and stare at the light.

- **Where to drop your line.** Fish can usually be caught around the bank where water meets land. They'll often hang where trees and bushes go out into or over the water. They will also work with the sun—in other words, if it's hot they will go to the shaded bank or the deeper water, and if it's cold they'll come to the shallows or sunnier water.

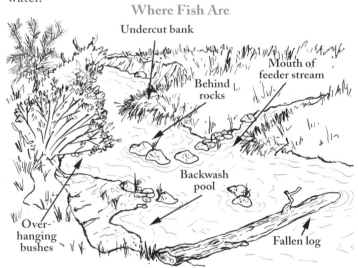

Where Fish Are

Undercut bank

Mouth of feeder stream

Behind rocks

Backwash pool

Over-hanging bushes

Fallen log

EATING PLANTS

If I haven't made it plain and clear before, let me do so now: **Eating unknown plants can be deadly!** Look at it this way, 90% of the plants on the planet are not edible for humans, but, conversely, 90% of the animal life is!

The other harsh fact is that plants simply don't give you enough bang for the buck. They do have nutrients in terms of vitamins, minerals, fiber, and maybe some starch and carbohydrate action, too. Such nutrition for the survivor is a secondary concern, whereas real energy in the form of calories is critical to the survivor and that comes best in the form of meat. But, if you find a lot of something, and it looks like it might yield a large amount of food, then the taste test comes into play. Of course this might warrant the ultimate risk factor—death.

Use all of your experience and common sense in trying to assess not only the quantity and quality of the potential food-source plant, but also its danger criteria. Use what you know to be good; and only after a taste test.

Does it look like anything you've seen in the store or restaurant before?

Does it look like any food source you've heard of or seen pictures of?

Maybe there was something like it in that crazy local market you visited the day before you got stranded out in the bush; maybe you saw the picture on a menu last week in that Asian restaurant. Bring it all to bear in evaluating the next steps, as it might save your life, or end it. Now let's talk about the real dealio with the UET. . . .

The Universal Edibility Test

The first thing to understand is that there is **no** failsafe universal test to see if something is edible or not. For example, there are plants that are fine when raw but kill if cooked, and vice versa. Likewise, there are exceptions for every rule out there for plants that are safe.

It is important to understand that the Universal Edibility Test (UET) really should be called the "Edibility

Test Universally *Applied*." That is its intended purpose and why it was designed by the military. They recognized that wars happen all over the globe and that it was not uncommon for soldiers, sailors, and airmen to get separated during the course of warfare and become isolated in remote regions where they might need to rely on the land for food.

So the military designed a "Universal Edibility Test" as a *guide* for soldiers to use to test unfamiliar local plant life and see if it was safe to eat or not. It's not infallible, nor is it the only way to go about it. Remember, humans have been trying foods forever and a day since the beginning of time, and that's really what it all comes down to—observation, common sense, and a calculated risk. So, let's look at some parameters to help you reduce the risk in the first place and then we'll discuss the UET by the "book" and its alternatives.

Understand that many people die every year from eating poisonous plants. It begins to border on "unintelligent" if you have animals around and the ability to catch and eat them. Almost all land animals are safe to eat, and once skinned and cooked, all of them are!

But let's say there just ain't no animals around, or you ain't caught none lately. When do you start eyeballin' plants to eat? Well, start eyeballing them right away. **always** be on the look out for chow!

First, look for anything familiar. If you know what something is for sure, or you find a plant that looks a whole lot like something you know is edible, then there is a chance it might be of the same family or a local variation of that edible plant. So, that's a good candidate for starters.

Next, make sure there's lots of it. This is really

important! No point in taking all that risk, and making all that effort, to get a handful of nibbles. If there aren't a whole lot of little things, or a few really big things, then it might not be worth the risk.

In general: Things that stink, sting, burn, or are barbed are usually not good candidates for the ol' taste test. *Exception*: prickly pears on cacti have mighty mean tiny spines but taste great and are very nutritious. Thistles are tricky ones, too, as are some of the crazier tropical fruits which have heavy "hornage" but juicy innards. Try to pay attention to all the exotic fruits and veggies in your grocers and markets to make a study of what some of these look like.

The taro leaf, for example, is a food staple for many indigenous folks in the oceanic areas, but it's a poisonous plant because it has *oxalate* crystals which look like barbed spikes under a microscope. However, boiling takes all that out and makes a yummy meal of it.

Plants to Avoid

- **Mushrooms.** These are tasty and they do have some (albeit very little) nutritional value, but the risks of eating any mushroom out in the wild is borderline suicidal! There are experts with years of study who still die from eating the wrong mushroom every year. For the survivor, mushrooms are simply OTL—Off the List!

Here's the kicker for mushrooms; they can taste fine and you think you're all good and they turn around and kill you 24 hours or even days later when it's way too late to do anything about it. If you're going to try and eat the things anyway, then do try and cook them. But know this: many fungal toxins are resistant even to high heat, and so cooking the shrooms will not always kill the toxins!

- **Shiny-leaved plants** are generally taboo, but not shiny like banana leaves, we mean shiny when they look like they have a sheen from a light coat of oil.

- **Yellow and white berries** are almost always bad juju, though there are exceptions. But for this book: if it's yellow, white, or even green, stay off it! (While we're on berries, the upside is that 90% of berries that are purple, blue, and black are good to go. Also, raspberries and similar "cluster or aggregate" berries are 99% safe.)

- **The rules for red berries are tricky.** We all know strawberries and cherries are yummy as are cranberries, raspberries, salmonberries, lingonberries, etc. However, many red berries are poisonous, so the guide here is like for mushrooms—if you don't know it, don't eat it. Holly berries are red and juicy but these are toxic, whereas Hawthorne berries are dry but healthy. *Yes, I know the birds eat hollyberries!* But that doesn't make them any less toxic to humans. In general, if the critters can eat it, so can you. **but** that is not the rule because some animals have immunities to these toxins.

Berry rules:
90% of purple, black & blue are good for you.
90% of yellow and white just aren't right.
50/50 on the reds—could be good, or could be dead.
If singletons or cluster berries, eating them could be merry.
But if they grow in a one-stem batch, best not put them down the hatch.

Umbrella-shaped flowers are bad.

Plants with three-leafed growth patterns are bad. Some of these are also poisonous to the touch, such as poison ivy.

Milky or discolored sap is usually bad. One of the notable exceptions is coconut milk.

Beans, seeds, and pods are generally best avoided unless you know them.

Grains are tricky because often it takes too many and too much work to be worthwhile, but if you find any heads with a pink, purple, or black spur just leave them well enough alone.

Plants with a soapy or bitter taste are best left alone.

Fine hairs, spines, or thorns are signs of plants to avoid.

Plants that look like dill, parsley, carrot, and parsnip are often very poisonous.

An almond smell in plants in general almost always indicates it's poisonous. (The counter to this is the general rule that plants smelling of onions and garlic are usually safe to try.)

Mind the mangoes and cashews if you're highly sensitive to poison ivy and sumacs, as these have similar properties on their surfaces that can cause a bad reaction.

Try not to eat plants with worms as they are decayed—instead, eat the worms!

Burn, boil, wash, and peel! Try to peel everything first, wash everything you can't peel, and cook everything! Some plants from the water have giardia, and anything from the soil can have bacteria, fungus, and other parasites. So use these simple methods to best prepare your food for safe consumption.

Some plants, like acorns, are highly bitter due to tannin concentrations, but with a few boils and water changes, are excellent to eat. So, it's a bit of work and a learning game when it comes to plant selection and preparation. If you can't get fire, try rinsing in water and drying in the sun.

Now, the **Universal Edibility Test**. The column on the left is the U.S. Army Survival Manual procedure. On the right is my test method, comments and observations based on experience and application.

Edibility Test

Military Edibility Test	Hawke Taste Test
Test only one part of the plant at a time.	This is absolutely correct, but also neglects the common sense test. Most folks aren't going to arbitrarily take a plant and mix it up and try and eat a salad.
Separate all the components—leaves, stalk, roots, flowers, fruit, buds, etc.	This too, tends to overlook the obvious. For most survivors who are starving, they aren't looking for all the parts to eat, they want that one edible part.
Smell for strong or acid odors; this alone can not be relied upon.	There are some good foods that are stinky, but mostly, smell will tell you if you're on the right track or not.
Do not eat for eight hours beforehand	If you are starving, you probably haven't eaten for a little more than eight hours. The point is to have an empty stomach for the best "thorough" analysis of the potential food source as viable or not. Most people will surely be here by the time they're

	ready to risk their life by eating unknown plants.
During this time, test for any contact reactions by placing the part to be tasted against your inner wrist or elbow for about 15 minutes.	Touch it to the outer part of your forearm first, if no reaction there, then try the inner part— if it does flame up, the outer hurts a whole lot less. Nothing wrong with waiting 15 minutes, but really, five will give you a good enough indicator if it's gonna burn or not.
Scratch Test addition: Scratch a piece of your flesh with your nail and see if rubbing the potential food on that causes a reaction or irritation.	Some folks say to actually scratch yourself, and that is an option to be extra safe, but if you got dirty fingernails and you're in the tropics, I don't recommend tearing holes into your only layer of protection from infection.
During the test, eat nothing except the part being tested, and purified water.	Well, if you got purified water, you're already doing ok. The other point is common sense, but it is valid: if you got other food, stay off it while testing so as to not mix or dilute your test results.
Take a portion of the part of the plant you plan to eat and prepare it the way you plan to eat it.	Mostly, if you got fire, cook or boil everything! No reason not to do so and lots of reasons to do so. Yes, cooking or boiling might take away some nutrients, but it will also take away more bacteria and toxins, which will hurt you a lot more. Boil if you can as that makes a broth you can drink to stay

	hydrated with clean water and still get some of those nutrients from the broth. But if you have nothing and no fire, then this test will be done in the "raw." But do rinse or peel whenever possible.
Before tasting the prepared plant part, touch a small portion to your lip and see if it burns or itches.	Yep, this is rock solid, do it!
If after three minutes there is no reaction, place a pinch on your tongue and hold it there 15 minutes.	This is pretty good, though I think you'll know sooner than three minutes. One minute is likely okay for the first touch, but the 15 minutes on the tongue is a bit much. I say five minutes is good. You'll know if it's not right pretty quickly as you'll be so hungry and your juices will be flowing, so reactions will be much more concentrated and quicker.
If there is no reaction, chew it thoroughly for 15 minutes, but do not swallow.	Again, I say five minutes is all you need.
If there is no burning, itching, stinging, inflammation or other reaction, then swallow and wait eight hours.	Yep, if so far so good, swallow and wait. But I'd say, based on your sense of the food, closely resembling a plant you know or think you know, or if it's radically alien to you, wait up to two hours, four hours tops, though 90% of the time you'll

	know in the first hour or so.
If anything goes wrong, isn't right, or there is any negative reaction at all, induce vomiting and drink lots of water.	Yes, and consider some of the ash, charcoal diarrhea drinks as neutralizers too (see First Aid chapter). For emergency medicine, charcoal is used for poisonings when vomiting isn't possible or warranted.
If nothing happens, then eat ¼ cup's worth of the prepared plant part.	Or thereabouts; eat a decent amount but don't gorge yourself yet. If it's not good, it would be worse to have a belly full of it. So, go easy for starters.
Wait eight hours; if nothing happens, the plant part as prepared is safe to eat.	Again, wait awhile, two-to-four hours and you should know. Take a nap, get up, and move around a bit to see if activity induces nausea. But if all seems good, it's likely ok.
Army says the UET takes 24 hours.	**Hawke** says it takes eight hours.

Universal Edibles

- **Fruits, nuts, and berries** are found all over the planet. Even in the Arctic it is possible to dig up berries from under the snow. The problem is that they come in so many shapes and sizes and colors. So, all one can do is to be on the lookout for anything that looks like these things, and then apply the rules of the UET:

   Amount: Are there lots to eat, or are they big enough to make a real meal from a few?

   About: Do they look like something you know or have seen before?

In Doubt: Do any warning signs—smell, touch, taste, look—call it into doubt?

If in doubt, throw it out!

Also keep an eye out for the critters around you. Are they nibbling on something?

- **Roots, tubers, and other stuff to dig up.** Anything you dig up should be cooked if at all possible. Not only is there concern about ground bacteria, fungi, and other evil spores, but the real deal is that roots are a concentrate of everything that's in the plant as its storage facility. So, boiling or cooking can neutralize any toxins or otherwise strong concentrations that might cause you some grief.

- **Grass, greens, shoots, stems and all in between.** Many plants that grow in and around water are edible. Also, people can eat grasses—not a lot, and they should only be the brightest green, newly fresh grasses, but they can be eaten—they are not dangerous and have some nutritional value.

  Many trees have brand new stems that are edible, or, when small little saplings are coming up out of the ground, they are often edible as well. Always apply the UET.

- **Eating trees!** You can actually eat a good many trees!

  For example, the spruce tree buds, needles, and stems can all be eaten raw, but they're better cooked. Many fresh baby sproutlings can be nibbled on from a lot of trees like the evergreen (green year round) coniferous (plants with cones) pines.

  Birch, spruce and other trees have an inner bark that is edible. This inner bark is thicker and richer in spring and summer than winter but is edible year round. See the list of edible plants by region for a better idea, but many hard woods do have some sort of edible inner bark, many winter trees have nuts, and many spring trees have edible shoots.

Regional Factors

Desert

- **Cacti** are all over most deserts and they're mostly edible. If you chop into them and they're green, they're good to go! If they have a white sap, don't rule them out right away—smell, finger-touch, lip-touch, and/or tongue-touch the sap. If no bad smell or burn, go easy at first; but figure it's likely ok. But if it don't look right, forget it.

- **Agave and yucca flower and stalks** are good to eat and provide a decent meal. Cut off about three feet of the bud and stalk (which looks like a huge asparagus tip), peel the hard outside, and eat raw, or any way you please. The flowers of both are edible raw, but cooked is better as the yucca flower tastes soapy (in fact it can be used to make soap).

  The fruit of both can be eaten as well, and it's best to eat while white inside. You can cut the agave down to its middle section and dig a hole that fills with water. After drinking, cut it off and cook it for a few hours—the agave is like a big potato, and the yucca roots are also just like potatoes.

- **Date palm** is a good find. They look like the obvious palm tree but instead of large nuts, you'll see clusters of small round fruit. The best way to get at them is to cut the tree down. If you should happen upon these fruits—which are like coconuts and bananas—in the jungle, you'll know what to do and enjoy.

- **Acacia** are those little trees with the thorny spines and nice yellow flowers that smell good. These trees are all over the world in good quantities, and the best part is, a tree can feed you a whole meal as the flowers, the buds, and the young leaves are all good to eat.

- **Amaranth** is found all over the world as well. It is full of vitamins and minerals, and when found, it is usually in abundance. It can be eaten raw or cooked. It is also known in:

  Africa: Vegetable for all, or *yoruba*

  Asia: Different names all over, but the Chinese call it *yin choi*

  Latin America and Caribbean: Here it's called *callalou*

  US: Chinese spinach

Sea

- **Seaweeds, kelp, samphire** and pretty much anything green from the sea or near the sea can be eaten. The seaweeds and kelps can be eaten raw in a pinch, but only take small amounts unless or until you can cook or boil them. Many of the harder shoreline plants are also edible, but best boiled. In general, most sea greens are fairly safe to munch, just make sure they're healthy and still anchored in somewhere. The only poisonous one you might encounter looks feathery, not leafy. Do not eat any sea plants that are colorful.

  Ideally you'll want to boil your sea greens to reduce the salt, kill any bacteria and parasites, and generally make them more palatable. If you don't have fire, try rinsing well in fresh water if available and letting it dry in the sun. They can cause a laxative effect if too much is eaten without anything else in the stomach.

Arctic

Most of the mosses that you find on trees or the ground, and the lichens you find growing on rock, are all edible. In a pinch, these can be eaten raw, but are best boiled.

- **Arctic willow** is a plant that you pretty much will only get to chow on its tender little sprouts in spring.

- **All pines and spruce** are edible, and the same rules for eating apply to both. The needles are edible and make fine, nutritious tea. The inner bark is edible, as are the baby cones, as well as the pine nut seeds from young cones in spring. Most parts are almost always better boiled.

- **The fern** is a fine plant for eating. But only eat the freshly sprouted tips that look like their nickname: "fiddle heads." These can be eaten raw, but are also better and safer to eat any quantity after boiling.

Forests & Mountains

- **Oaks, pines, and beechwood** all have edible inner bark, and for all the evergreens (except the yew, which has flat needles instead of round ones) you can eat the raw needles, baby cones, and seeds from the cones. The deal for eating bark is to peel off the brown stuff from the tree, then find a thin layer of slightly slimy but meaty bark, kind of like an inner skin—this is what you peel and eat. Not the dry outer bark, and not the hard wood inside. It will always taste funny, it's a tree! But it is edible and nutritious and filling. It is harsh on the trees, so try not to "ring" them, but that is survival.

- **Plants like burdock, plantain, cattail, arrowroot, dandelion, sorrel, and sassafras** are all good finds as food sources.

- **Pokeweed** is poisonous if not boiled, but one plant provides a lot of food.

- **Purslane** grows everywhere, often in open sunny areas. It is a thick, fleshy-leaf plant with all parts being edible raw or cooked.

- **Chicory** is one of my faves for making field coffee. To do this, roast the roots until dry and dark brown, then crush and use like coffee. Just look for the sky-blue dandelion-like flower on the base of the stem with milky juice. You're in there! Grows all over the world and all parts are edible.

- **Thistle** is good when you peel and boil the stalk, and eat the roots raw or cooked. It can usually be found in dry woods. It can be eaten raw as well as the flowers and leaves.

- **Wild onion and garlic, wild rose, and water lily** are good for starters. These are found most anywhere in such regions. For the few you might not be so sure about, look them up before you travel as they're very common, and once you know them, you'll always know them.

- **Cattails** are my favorite as they are near almost all swamps and ponds and small stream areas, and they offer so much food in that all of it is edible at various parts of the year—raw if you must, but boiled or roasted over the fire, these are great grubs.

- **Dandelion** roots and heads and leaves are good to eat—just discard the stems with their milky white sap (which makes a decent glue). They're good to eat raw or cooked.

But try not to eat a lot at one go just because you found a field of them—tummy upset is likely to result if you do.

Jungle

- **Palms** are a good food source. Cut the tops off and eat the tips, the soft parts, the flowers, the seeds, and the heart of the palm. If small, dig into the ground to get the heart found in the root.

- **All nuts** you can find are not only a great source of food, but they are excellent travel food as they'll last for months in their shells. So save these up for any journeys being planned. If you do find a lot of nuts, you can squeeze the oils out of them by wrapping them in a strong cloth and beating them and then using something to "press" the oils out. You can use the oils for your skin, cooking, candles, etc. Also, use the oil cloth as your wick for you oil candle.

- **Coconuts** are an excellent source of food and water. Use a sharpened stick placed in the ground as a sort of spike to stab the coconut onto, and wedge the husk off with lever action. Then, 2-3 whacks on the sides of the coconut around the middle will get it to split open.

- **Bananas** are another great source of food. Easy to access and plenty filling, and the banana tree itself is a fantastic source of water as well.

- **Indian Grass** is another plant found readily in many warmer climates. The key to ID is simple—if you see a clump of fat stalked grasses, these are likely to be lemon grasses. Simply pluck one and taste—if sour, it's lemon.

- **Papayas** are super to find because they are so huge that one will fill you up.

- **Bamboo** is also awesome to find for the absolute

all-purpose utility of it. The baby shoots can be eaten raw, although they can be bitter. Boil with a few changes of water to make them a lot nicer tasting.

- **Sugar cane** is not a likely find, but it is all over the tropics as a remnant from failed plantations.

- **Taro** is found all over in the tropics; it has to be boiled to neutralize the oxalates. Once that's done, the leaves and the roots provide super tasty greens and starches.

- **Water lilies** are plentiful but it can be hard to get out there to pull up their tuber roots. Once done, boil or roast.

- **Sops** are some crazy-looking fruit to most Americans. They are mainly in the tropics of Asia and there are two kinds—sweet and sour. They are tasty and plentiful.

Eating Bugs

Bugs are everywhere on the planet, and since they are often at the bottom of the food chain, that means there are more of them than anything else. So, they are more plentiful than the animals and a whole lot easier to catch. They are also more plentiful than edible plants and provide a whole lot more energy and nourishment than the plants.

So bugs become, by simple math, one of your best survival food resources, period.

Bug Nutrition

While hunting is the best way when able, it would be foolish to ignore insects as a food source and a good supplement to any diet out in the wild.

For 100 grams of lean ground beef, you get about 28 grams of protein and no fat.

For 100 grams of broiled cod fish, you get about 27 grams of protein and no fat.

Now look at comparable protein and fat statistics per 100 grams of the following insects:

Bug Nutrition*

Insect	Protein	Fat
Grasshoppers	20	6
Beetles	19	8
Termites	14	0
Ants	13	3
Crickets	12	5
Worms	9	5
Caterpillars	6	0

*Compiled from studies from Africa, Mexico, Iowa and Wisconsin.

Making the case for bug eating even stronger is the fact that, while bugs might not have all the protein of the pure meats of the fish and cow, they do have more fat and that makes them actually better for surviving than the pure proteins with *no* fats.

Taking it one step further, and putting to rest the issue of "can you or can't you bring yourself to eat bugs" once and for all, the bugs come with a lot of other minerals, vitamins, and nutrients that the pure meats don't provide. Since an insect is a complete life form, it stands to reason it would have a more complete amount of nutrition provided by its complete consumption.

In short, bugs are probably one of the best survival foods if you can get enough of them. If the quantities are lacking, then use them as you catch them to supplement your diet. That said, let's look at the rules for eating them.

Bug Dining Rules

- **Beetles, caterpillars, ants, crickets, grasshoppers, cockroaches, etc.**—all the commonly known insects—are pretty much fair game.

  The general rule is if they are brightly colored, smell foul, have spikes or barbs, or bite, then you might want to avoid them, but that doesn't necessarily rule them out. Remember, everything has exceptions!

  It's almost always better to boil them or roast them on a hot rock by the fire or on a stick. Remove anything hard like shells, legs, wings, pincher heads and stinger tails.

- **Hairy insects** should be squashed and the guts thrown into the broth for boiling; or burn the hairs off with the flames.

- **Spiders** are edible, but they're really not worth the time or risk as you usually only get one at a time. However if you find a huge tarantula, then chuck him in the stew.

- **Scorpions** can also be scarfed. Just be careful, remove the stinger, cook when you can.

- **Bees** are very nutritious and often come in bunches. There are two tricks to eating bees. One, you must kill them before they kill you. And two, you must remove their stingers before eating them. To kill them, use smoke, and try to go after their nest at night. They'll be less inclined to attack then. Smoke them out by putting some good smokey material in their hole and sealing it. Then check the next day, being ready with more smoke. If they're dead, scoop out the score. The honey is delicious and nutritious and you can eat the comb or use it as a wax for other things like candle light or water sealant. If you have a known allergy to bee stings, then stay outta the honey pot!

- **Slugs, snails and worms** are all edible, but they require an extra step. Soak them for a day or so in water to get them to purge their guts, then cook them up well. Again, anything brightly colored, especially around the sea, is likely dangerous and is better to leave well enough alone.

6

TOOLS

The first thing you do in a survival situation is to make an inventory of what you **do** have.

WEAPONS FIRST

There are absolutely two things that must be with any survivor at all times: a stick and a knife.

The Stick

Things to consider in attaining a good survival stick:
Find one that is about 6-12 inches taller than you.
Look for the straightest, strongest one you can find.
Use a manmade material if it's available, like a pipe or metal rod.
For your best bet, find a strong sapling tree that you can cut to fit.
Select a stick just big enough that when you grasp it, your fingers and thumb touch
Choose a stick with a natural fork at the top (or make one).
Carve a point at the bottom.

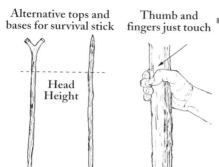

Alternative tops and bases for survival stick

Thumb and fingers just touch

Head Height

The survival stick

- **Height.** Choose a stick slightly taller than you; if the stick is too short, it may jam into your neck if you fall. It can serve as a measuring device—how deep a river is or could you jump over a chasm? If the stick is strong enough, it might even be used as a small bridge. It can be used as a rafting pole, a crutch, a spear, a reaching tool and digging tool, etc.

The Knife

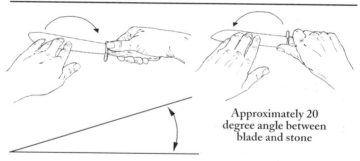

Approximately 20 degree angle between blade and stone

Knife sharpening

If you have one, that's great. If not, improvise one ASAP as it is simply the most valuable tool for survival. Bones, wood, metal, glass, shells and bamboo can be made into knives.

Other Potential Weapons

Now that we've covered the basics of the two mainstays in the armament of the survivor—sticks and knives—let's take a look at other potential weapons.

- **Dirt** In a pinch, you can grab a handful of dirt and throw it at a predator or game.

    You can fill a sack or t-shirt with dirt and use it as a rock-like weapon: aim for the eyes.

- **Rocks** These were probably the very first weapon humans used.

- **Throw sticks** are like a non-returning boomerang. Sharpen points onto both ends of the stick and use a straight stick if that is all you have.

- **Clubs** The best are usually the harder woods so they don't snap on impact.

- **Spears** These have been around for time immemorial. The basic spear is just a long, strong stick with a sharp point at the end. In its simplest form it is best used for lunging and piercing mid-sized game such as a small pig or doe. It takes some skill to effectively throw a spear. Because the standard spear is best for lunging and not for throwing, they should be very strong.

    Making a spear is simple, but if possible, you should fire-harden it.

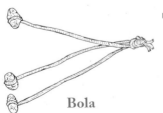

Bola

- **Bolas** are effective weapons for hunting. Three rocks tied to three strings which are tied together at the other end. The bola is swung overhead and thrown at the prey.

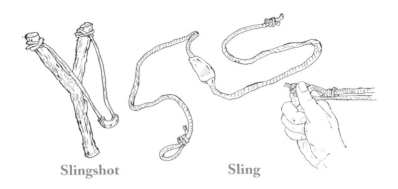

Slingshot   Sling

- **Slingshots** Most people know what a slingshot is from childhood.

     Before you start hunting, practice for awhile to increase your accuracy and velocity.

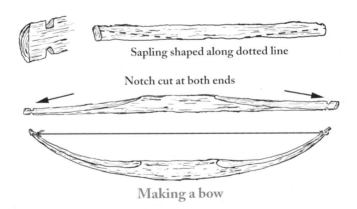

Sapling shaped along dotted line

Notch cut at both ends

Making a bow

- **Bow and Arrow** The bow and arrow are the classic weapons of the primitive world. They are time-intensive to make, but they can improve your mammal-hunting success.

- **Nets** If you have time, patience, and cordage, then make a net as great multi-purpose tool. Nets can be used for catching fish, snaring birds, trapping small game, as a hammock to sleep in, as a litter for a patient, or as a rucksack to carry your goods on the move.

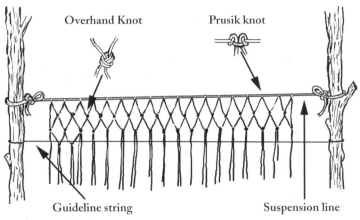

Making a net

Tools

Utensils

You will need something to help you eat. This keeps dirty fingers out of your food.

Always make some type of fork, spoon or chopstick.

Baskets and Other Carrying Tools

Whenever possible, keep it simple by using your shirt, poncho, coat, or blanket. If you don't have these, make a basket, and reeds are good for these purposes.

- **Backpack Frames** will let you carry more weight, more easily. There are three easy ways to make a simple backpack frame:

The **"Wishbone"**, the **"A-frame"**, and the **"Square"** frame. Just fashion the sticks like the name and fasten them together, make straps and you're set.

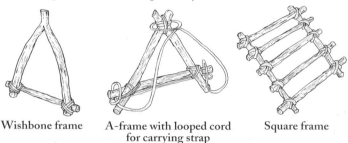

| Wishbone frame | A-frame with looped cord for carrying strap | Square frame |

Backpack frames

Bowls

Bowls are a fundamental implement. You can make a bowl out of a closed-ended segment of bamboo, or from a block

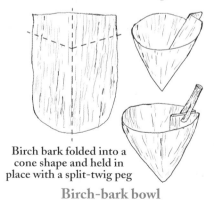

of wood using fire coals to burn out the center. Tree barks—such as birch—are good for bowls. A piece of birch can be peeled off and rolled up into a cone, or actually folded into a box shape. Then take a small twig, form it into a one-inch peg, split it

Birch bark folded into a cone shape and held in place with a split-twig peg

Birch-bark bowl

halfway down the middle, and slide it over the edges of the bark like a paper clip and it will hold your utensil in its shape.

If you can't find bark or leaves to shape into a cone and use as a bowl, try making a mud bowl. Then fire the bowl—this will make it tougher.

Boats and Rafts

If you're going to make a raft, find the lightest wood you can. Tap all the trees around you and find the lightest, softest ones. Without an axe or machete, you won't be able to cut fresh trees and will be stuck having to find what you can lying around.

Use as many as long logs as you need, but one can work, select them large enough to hold your weight. **Do not** raft at night. **Do** stay to the inside of river bends. **Do not** attempt to navigate rapids.

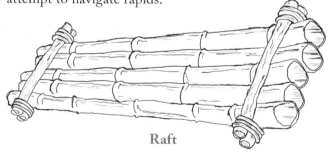

Raft

- **River Crossing.** River crossing **alone** can be very dangerous. Use ropes, anchors and floats whenever you can, consider natural bridges or avoidance.

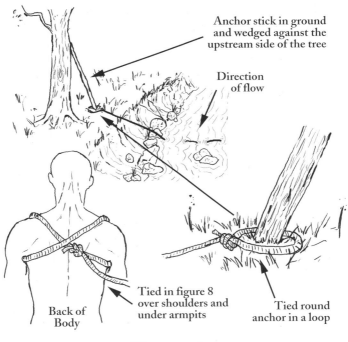

Anchor stick in ground and wedged against the upstream side of the tree

Direction of flow

Tied in figure 8 over shoulders and under armpits

Back of Body

Tied round anchor in a loop

River crossing

- **In a cold environment, avoid getting your boots wet at all costs, or your only clothes.** Get nekkid, get across, get dry again. Stay warm, stay alive. Getting wet is getting dead.

Rope and Cordage
Rope is another important item to have in a survival situation. If you have it, keep it, if not, consider making it. Bark, roots, vines and grasses can be made into cordage.

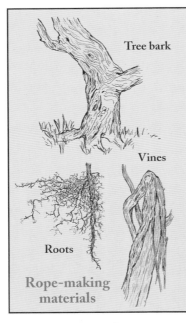

Facts about using natural fibers for making cordage:

Anything green and pliable is possible to use.
If material is dry, and in the winter, soak the material in water.
When a fiber is really hard to work with, boil it.
Test everything with your eyes and hands to see if it's usable before you start working it.
Test everything after you make it to ensure it's still usable.

Tree bark

Vines

Roots

Rope-making materials

How to Make Rope and Cordage

Once you have the base material fibers selected and prepared, you're ready to begin.

Take several strands and tie a small knot at one end. Then twist these fibers together to make a strong strand, and knot the other end.

Repeat the last step until you have a good number of strands to work with.

Next, take two of the strong strands you just made, and begin to braid them together by criss-crossing them in an overlapping fashion until you get to the ends.

Make a knot at the other end.

If you need longer cordage, tie two more strands to that end, and start the braiding process again.

That's about all on the basics of making any cordage. You'll use what you have, make what you can, and make it as strong as you need.

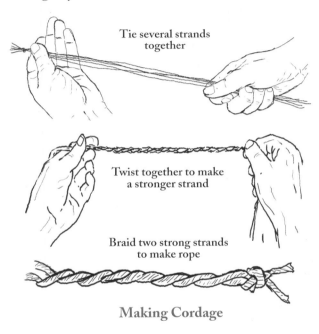

Tie several strands together

Twist together to make a stronger strand

Braid two strong strands to make rope

Making Cordage

Knots

Everything you need can be managed with a granny knot—it's as easy as tying your shoes. To make life easier, a few more knots are helpful.

Overhand knot

- **Overhand Knot** This is the simplest knot. It's the common knot you make in a single rope to keep the end from fraying, for example. Just make a loop in one end of the string, then pass the other end through the loop and pull tight.

- **Half Hitch Knot** This one is pretty simple, too. It can be used 90% of the time for almost everything. Simply wrap the string around the object, tuck it in on itself, and pull tight.

Half hitch knot

- **Square Knot** This is a bit trickier. It's really good for binding two pieces of cordage together.

They say it's not good when joining two ropes of unequal diameter. I say use it even then, just put a half hitch on each end afterwards and it'll hold.

Square knot

To make a square knot, just remember: **over-under, under-over:**

Hold one piece in one hand, the other piece in the other hand. Lay one side over the other, it doesn't matter which. Then take that same piece and turn it under the other. Turn it back pointing towards its original start point. Then bring it back under the other string.

Then wrap it back around over the other string.

Pull them together slowly and dress them up a bit as they come together.

They should form a sort of symmetrical square, hence the name: square knot.

- **Granny Knot** is similar to the square knot, except the sequence is: **right over left, right over left**—or **left over right, left over right.**

- **Prusik Knot** is basically another form of a half hitch. It is ideal for tying into other ropes without cutting up your cordage. It is good for making a slip knot, as well for emergency ascents.

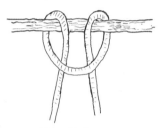

Prusik knot

It makes a bight that won't slide under tension, but when loosened it can be slid around and moved easily to a new place on the rope.

To make a prusik knot:

Make a bight or loop or upside-down "U" with your string. Make it a few inches long so you can work with it.

Place it over the rope or object you want to tie into/onto.

Then pull the rest of your string through that bight so that it's wrapped around the rope.

Then dress it up so it looks neat like a letter "T" across the rope.

Pull tight to lock in; loosen to move or slide.

That's it, all the knots you need to know.

7

NAVIGATION

NUMBER ONE QUESTION IN SURVIVAL: "SHOULD I STAY OR SHOULD I GO?"

If you are with a vehicle or craft, 90% of the time, you will be better off staying. Rescue teams go to the survivor's last known location and begin searching where they were supposed to be if they left some sort of plan. But sometimes you need to go.

Choosing to move raises other questions. Do you know which way to go? How far it is? Do you have the resources, internal and external, to overcome the terrain, the weather, the distance, to get there?

While staying put and waiting for help to find you is often your best option, certain circumstances can force you to find your own way out.

Stay Where You Are If:

You are with a plane, boat, or other vehicle.

You are at a shelter.

You are with a group.

(Unless any of the above is in danger of sinking, exploding, burning down, or falling off a cliff.)

Prepare to Depart If:

You are completely lost and far from anything man-made.

You are alone and no one has any clue where you are.

You are almost certain no one will be looking for you, or they won't begin looking for a long time, or they won't be looking in the right place because you're not where anyone would expect you to be, or you've waited as long as you can at the boat, car, plane, or house.

You are running out of supplies.

A member of your party requires emergency medical care.

The Basics

■ **Dead reckoning** is the simplest and most effective style of survival navigation. It works in all types of terrain. Simply look in the direction you want to travel. Pick the farthest "target" or landmark object that you can see and begin walking toward it.

Be sure to estimate the distance before you begin, and be sure to take a pace count as you go (see below). Shortly after you set off toward your objective, turn around and look at your starting point for a moment to consider what it will look like from the perspective of your destination.

When you get to your target, you can look back, and see where you came from, confirming that it's on-line and that you're on track. Then pick your next target and repeat.

If you can, try to line up three destinations in your sights. If all three landmarks are in line, then you are dead on track.

- **Orienteering.** For the purposes of survival, we'll define orienteering as navigating with a compass but without a map. You may not have a map for reference, but you can use your compass to maintain your bearings and direct your movements.

- **Terrain Association.** The art of navigating with a map, but without a compass, is called terrain association. This is a bit trickier, but also has its advantages. With a map, you have a good sense of the overall picture, and a much better sense of where you want to go, but it's not always so easy to know exactly where you are.

Maps—How to Read, Use, & Make Them

If you have a map, use it. If not, consider making one. Just trying to make your own map can force you to visualize your surroundings from a bird's-eye view. It's a good exercise, if nothing else, and can help you develop a better sense of awareness of your surroundings, which can give you peace of mind.

The simplest form of homemade map is a **sand table**. This is just making a model of the surrounding terrain in sand or dirt, using sticks as small trees and pebbles as rocks, whatever is available as a visual aid.

To make one, simply orient whatever you intend to write on toward the north and then build the map with your camp at the center. Add key terrain features and significant landmarks as you scout the area and discover new elements of your environment.

Terms & Concepts

- **Scale.** A map's scale tells you the size of the area it represents. More specifically, it tells you the size of the area

3 maps showing Houston, Texas on 3 different scales

Map Scales

represented by each of the map's squares. The scale can be found in the legend at the bottom or at the side of the map.

Many civilian maps are made by the U.S. Geological Survey at a scale of 1:24,000, where 1 inch on the map equals 24,000 inches on land. One square on this map is one square inch, and one inch represents 2,000 feet. These maps cover an area of 7.5 minutes of longitude by 7.5 minutes of latitude.

Most military maps use the metric system, which is more internationally applicable, and are drawn to a scale of 1:50,000. On these maps, the squares are one kilometer to a side. The distance from one corner of this square diagonally to another corner would be 1.5 kilometers, or "clicks."

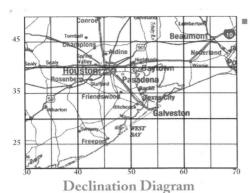

■ **Grid Coordinates.** Grids are formed by the vertical and horizontal lines drawn on the map, much as the lines of longitude and latitude divide the globe into square sections.

Declination Diagram

Locations on a map are expressed in grid coordinates.

■ **Legend.** A map's legend is like a book's table of contents and index all rolled into one. The legend will tell you the map's scale, where and when it was made, and all the visual keys you'll need to understand the map's symbols.

Map Legend

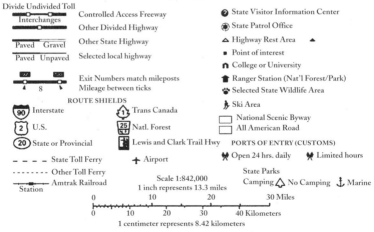

Some things are considered standard on a map:
Green = Vegetation (white areas contain few or no plants).
Blue = Water (rivers, lakes, intermittent streams, marshes, etc.).
Brown = Contour lines (which indicate elevation).
Red = Roads (or place names or major destinations like airports, etc.).
Black = Man-made structures (buildings, cemeteries, roads, etc.).
Black dashes usually mean some sort of trail. Blue dashes mean intermittent stream. It might be dry, but it's a good place to dig for water.

- **Coordinates.** These are the numbers used to pinpoint a location.

If a map starts at 25 at the bottom left corner and goes to 75 at the bottom right, then one of the 50 squares in between includes your east-west position. If the map's

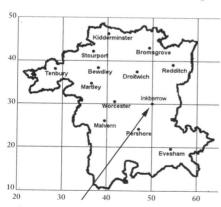

vertical coordinates start in the bottom left-hand corner at 10 and go up to 60, your north-south position would fall somewhere in one of those 50 squares.

To name your position, read right until you find the grid coordinate that corresponds to your east-west position,

Coordinates right 50 and up 30 give the location of Inkberrow

Map Coordinates

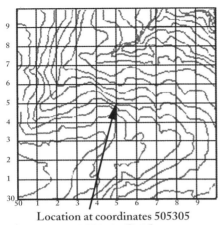

Location at coordinates 505305
6-Digit Grid

then read up until you reach the coordinate that corresponds to your north-south position.

When giving or receiving coordinates on a map, remember: Right & Up. This is simply a standardized way of reading or describing a location in a way that someone else can find it. Right gives the east-west coordinate, which comes first. Up gives the north-south coordinate.

Say your position is 50 and 30. On a military-style map of 1:50,000 scale, this would place you in the map's middle square. But that square represents one square kilometre. That's a lot of terrain in the middle of the jungle.

To mark the location more precisely, divide the square into 10 equal divisions. Since our square is 1,000 meters by 1,000 meters, dividing it into tenths narrows our square areas to 100 square meters. So the new way to describe the more detailed coordinate would be as follows: Right 50 then, say, 5, then up 30, then, say, 5 again. It would look like this: 505305. This coordinate will bring you within 100 meters of your desired location.

At this distance you could make contact by hollering. Mission accomplished. This is called a "6-digit" grid, and it's about the best you can do without a protractor.

Not bad for map-reading 101. With some practice, you

can get good at guesstimating an 8-digit coordinate, which will bring you to within 10 meters of your target. At this distance, you should be able to see your objective.

- **Contour Lines.** Each contour line, often a wavy brown line on the map, represents a consistent elevation, which will be indicated on the line. The contour interval is the distance between contour lines, and tells you how steep or how flat the terrain is. This will come into play when you plan your route.

    If the lines are close together, the elevation changes a lot in a very short distance, which means the terrain is steep. If the lines are farther apart, that means elevation change in the area is gradual.

Use the contour lines for following purposes:

To avoid peaks (or to find them if you need the vantage point for scouting).
To avoid steep valleys (or to find them if you're looking for water).
To avoid steep ridges, cliffs, or mountainsides.
To seek flat ground for ease of travel.

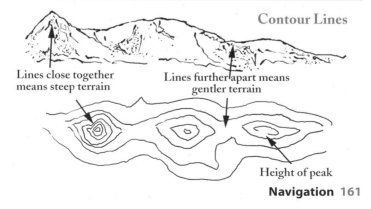

Contour Lines

Lines close together means steep terrain

Lines further apart means gentler terrain

Height of peak

In a survival situation, you just need to be aware that over long distances, it is normal that you will find yourself off-course. Don't panic or give in to disorientation and confusion.

The declination diagram shows you the differences between:
True north (often indicated by a line with a star).
Grid north (often indicated by a line with a square).
Magnetic north (often indicated by a line with an arrow or point).
Declination diagrams are drawn in the form of a "V" displaying the arc and variance between each arm of the "V." True north is not relevant here. What's important is the G-M (grid to magnetic) angle.
When you draw a line on a map from where you are to where you want to be, that line is called the grid azimuth.
We use the G-M angle to convert the map or "Grid" azimuth to the compass or "Magnetic" azimuth.
The acronym "LARS" is the easiest way to remember how to convert a G-M angle from Grid for plotting to Magnetic for walking: Left = Add; Right = Subtract
Depending on where you are in the world, the G-M angle could be left, or west, of the grid line, or it could be right, or east, of the grid line.
If the "M," or magnetic line, is left of the "G" or grid line, then you would add the number of the G-M angle.
That's how you take a plot from a map and apply it to a compass. To go from compass to map, reverse it.

Compasses

A compass relies on the laws of physics to tell you which direction is north. It is up to you to determine where you go in relation to that.

The Parts of a Compass

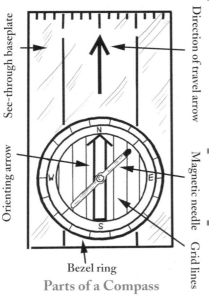

See-through baseplate

Orienting arrow

Direction of travel arrow

Magnetic needle

Grid lines

Bezel ring

Parts of a Compass

- **Bezel Ring.** Your compass has a ring around the outside that turns, called a bezel ring. When you turn the bezel ring, it makes a little click, and each click represents 3 degrees.

- **Scale.** Many modern compasses have a measuring tool, called a scale.

- **See-through back.** Many modern camping compasses have a see-through back so you can better orient your map.

How to Use a Compass

Hold the compass level to the ground so the needle can spin freely. Some compasses have a plumb bubble to help you keep the compass level. Keep the bubble in the center to ensure an accurate reading. Also, be sure to keep the compass away from metal objects, like watches or belt buckles.

Compass is held level to the ground and close to the eye

Using a Compass

Let the arrow spin until it settles in one direction. This is north. Turn your body so that you are facing north. You are now oriented to your environment. The arrow, the lines on the bezel and your nose should all be pointing in the same direction.

The compass face is divided with marks into degrees. There are 360 degrees. The **azimuth** is the direction you want to travel. North is an azimuth of 0 degrees. East is an azimuth of 90 degrees. South is an azimuth of 180 degrees.

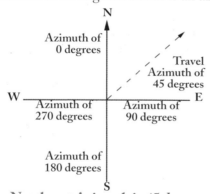

West is an azimuth of 270 degrees. **When you're facing north, your outstretched right hand points to 90 degrees, or due east. Your back is facing south and your left side faces west.**

Northeast Azimuth is 45 degrees

Here's an easy way to remember:
Nose = North
Right = East ("right-ist" or "right-ish")
Sit = South (your butt is south of your head)
Left = West (both words have an "E" so it's easy to remember)

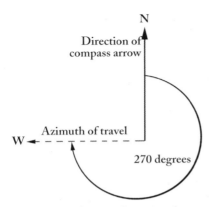

Due-West Azimuth is 270 degrees

The easiest way to maintain your sense of direction is to remember where the sun rose. The sun always rises in the east, so point your right shoulder toward where the sun came up and your nose will be facing north, your backside facing south, and your left to the west!

Let's say you are facing north, where your compass arrow is pointing. You know that civilization is to your west, or your left-hand side, about 500 miles or so. This means you want to travel on an azimuth of 270 degrees.

Set the azimuth on your compass by turning the compass body toward your target and line up the azimuth with the aiming points of your compass.

Keep the north-pointing arrow lined up between the bezel brackets (these are the two lines on the bezel that bracket the north-pointing arrow when the bezel is set at zero).

Now just face the direction of your pointers and walk your azimuth.

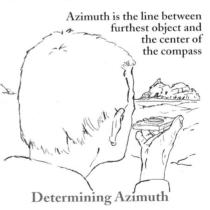

Azimuth is the line between furthest object and the center of the compass

Determining Azimuth

- **Back azimuth** simply defines the opposite direction of your azimuth. Let's say you are walking 90 degrees due east. Your back azimuth is 180 degrees opposite. By adding 180 degrees to your 90 degree azimuth, you get a back azimuth of 270 degrees. If your azimuth is greater than 180 degrees, then subtract 180 to get your back azimuth. An azimuth of 300 degrees would have a back azimuth of 120 degrees.

  Back azimuth comes in handy two ways. The first is in helping you find your way back to where you started, especially if you're just trying to get back to base camp after a day foraging. The second is to help you find your location on a map.

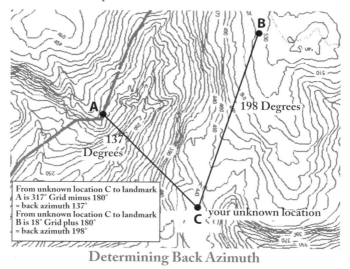

B

198 Degrees

A

137 Degrees

From unknown location C to landmark
A is 317° Grid minus 180°
= back azimuth 137°
From unknown location C to landmark
B is 18° Grid plus 180°
= back azimuth 198°

C your unknown location

Determining Back Azimuth

  The terms for this technique are "re-section" or "triangulation." If you have a map and a compass and don't know where you are, but you can see a landmark object in the distance, then you can "shoot" an azimuth at that object. Use that azimuth to determine a back azimuth, and draw that line on your map. Then shoot an azimuth at another distant point, maybe a mountaintop or ridge line. Then convert that to a back azimuth and draw another line on your map. The point where these two lines intersect pinpoints your location on the map. Now you know where you are.

Taking Directions from Nature

There are lots of myths about moss. Some books say moss grows facing the sun, and that moss will grow on the southern side of trees in the northern latitudes, since that's the side that gets the most sunlight. This is not always true.

The Moss Rules:
In the north, moss grows on the north side
In the south, moss grows on the south side
There ain't no rules!
It's not uncommon to find moss growing all the way around a tree.

- **Compass Plants.** These are plants that tend to be fairly good indicators of direction. They can be useful, if you know what they are and how to interpret them. Since most plants that grow at odd angles are doing so because they are trying to maximize their exposure to the sun, you can sometimes deduce direction from the way they lean. In the southern hemisphere, compass plants will tend to point north toward the sun. In the northern hemisphere, they'll be pointing south. Perennials tend to be thicker and lusher on the side that gets more sun, toward the equator.

How to Read the Sun, Moon, and Stars

The sun rises in the east and sets in the west. You can always find north by orienting your right shoulder toward the east, which points your nose north.

What Time Is It?

The 24-hour solar cycle is divided into day and night. These are roughly 12 hours each. You have to mentally calibrate according to your location and the season, but you can make a good guess at the time of day by where the sun is in the sky. When the sun is highest in the sky, it's noon. When it first rises, it's approximately 6 a.m. And when it sets, that is approximately 6 p.m.

A full moon can be used just like the sun—it rises in the east and sets in the west.

Telling time by the moon is a two-part process. First, look at how much of the moon is lit up. If half of the moon is lit, then the moon will be up half the night, or 6 hours. If one quarter is lit, it will be up only 3 of the night's 12 hours. If the moon is three-quarters lit, the moon will be up for 9 hours.

For the second part of the equation you have to know when the moon came up and where it is in the sky. You can guesstimate from there.

For example, if the moon is half full, you know it will be up for 6 of the night's 12 hours. If it came up at dusk, and is half way to the "high noon" position, then it's 9 p.m. If

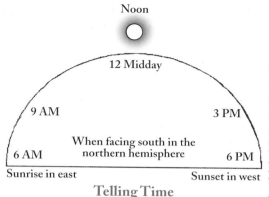

Telling Time

the moon didn't show up until midnight (you'll know this because it first appears in the high noon position) and the moon is only half lit, and it's halfway toward the horizon, or 6 a.m. position, then you know it's 3 a.m.

Knowing the time can help you plan your movements based on available light, and it also applies to navigation.

Traveling at Night

Generally speaking, you shouldn't travel at night. If you're stranded in the desert in the summer, when day movement will kill you, here's how to move at night without a compass.

- **Navigating by the Moon.** The moon orbits our planet about every 30 days. So we get approximately 1 week of full moon, 1 week of no moon, 1 week of half moon and 1 week of quarter moon. For a survivor planning to move at night, if you're facing nearly a week of fumbling in the dark, you must weigh very carefully the decision to move or not. Likewise, the full moon has a strong effect on tides and if your movement involves crossing water, this factor must be considered as well.

Telling the time by the moon is worked out by
how lit it is relevant to its position in the night sky

Moon Positioning

Now let's look at how the moon can be used for
navigating. If you look up at the sky in the early evening,
you will notice one of two things. Either the sun will go
down and there will be no moon until about midnight, or
the sun will be setting and you will see the moon is already
up. Here's what either case means to you:

If the moon doesn't come up until around midnight,
then the side that is lit is pointing east. Since the sun is

New   Young   Waxing   Waxing   Waxing
                  1 quarter   Half   3 quarters

full   Waning   Waning   Waning   old
        3 Quarters Half   1 Quarter

10 phases of the moon
(Waxing means increasing, Waning means decreasing)
Moon Phases

already down, you have only one celestial body to point the way. The phrase "one at least, to show the east" may help you remember.

If the moon is up at the same time as the sun, then the bright side of the moon is pointing to the west. Remember the phrase "two is best to show the west."

- **Orienting to a full moon.** When the moon is full, provided the sky is clear, you can use the **shadow tip method** (see p.173), just like with the sun, to orient yourself. Since the moon also rises in the east and sets in the west, all the same techniques apply.

- **Orienting to a crescent moon.** Regardless of which side of a crescent moon is lit, either will show you south. Just imagine a line from tip to tip of the crescent, and then continue that line down to the horizon, and that will point you generally due south every time. In the southern hemisphere, these will point you north.

Navigating by the Stars

- **The Big Dipper** stays in the position of true north throughout the year. It will always show north. It's one of the easiest-to-recognize constellations and points to the Pole Star or North Star.

  Find the Big Dipper, and trace from the handle down to the ladle and around the bottom of the ladle and up the front of the ladle to its upper lip. If you extend an imaginary line along the front of the ladle and out beyond its upper lip, that line will point the direction to the North or Pole Star.

- **The North Star** is actually the last star at the end of the handle of the Little Dipper.

  Look for the "W" of Cassiopeia. The middle point of the "W" points right at the Pole Star. Don't confuse the North Star with the planets Venus or Mars, which are very bright in the night sky and can be mistaken

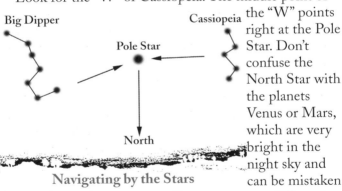

Navigating by the Stars

for stars by novice stargazers. One sure way to differentiate between them is that Mars is red and Venus is blue, and while both will be bright, neither will twinkle.

Once you have the North Star located, you will know for sure where north is, and you can determine the other directions from there. If you're headed east, keep the

North Star off your left shoulder, and you'll be facing and walking due east.

Getting Your Bearings in the Northern Hemisphere

This applies to most, as most of the earth's landmass is north of the equator. The lands south of the equator are often less populated and the most remote.

Always pay attention to where the sun came up and mark that location with a feature of the terrain. Since most survival movements are based on a general direction of travel, like north or south, instead of any precise angle of azimuth, all you really need to do is locate your cardinal directions.

Example: You see the sun rise over a mountain in the distance. That mountain is to your east. You know that a large city is somewhere to the south of you. So, you point your left shoulder toward that mountain and you're now facing south. As you walk, keep checking over your shoulder to make sure that the mountain is in the same relative position, to your left, and you'll know that you are still headed in a generally southerly direction. Make sure to use a fixed, identifiable feature of the terrain, the farther away the better. Do not use the sun as your reference feature, since it moves, and you'll end up going in a big U-turn.

During the daylight to figure out your direction without a compass, this is the most common and easy to use.

- **Shadow Tip Method.** As the sun rises in the east, it will cast a shadow pointing west. As the sun passes the high-noon position, toward the western horizon, the shadow will move to the opposite side, or toward the east.

So as the sun rises from east to west, it casts a shadow that moves west to east.

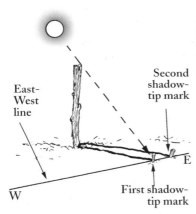

Shadow Tip Method

Find an open area, place about a 1-foot stick in the ground, and look to see where the shadow falls. Mark the tip of the shadow with a rock, a small stick, or a line in the dirt. Wait about 5 minutes while the tip of the shadow moves. Now, mark the new position of the shadow. Mark a line connecting the two positions. This is an accurate east-west line. Extend the line in the dirt about a foot to each side so it's long enough to stand on.

Put your left foot on the end nearest the first mark and your right foot on the end nearest the second mark. You are now facing north. Your left shoulder is pointing west, your right shoulder is pointing east, and south is behind you.

Getting Your Bearings in the Southern Hemisphere

- **During the Day.** The sun always rises in the east and sets in the west, so many aspects of navigating in the northern hemisphere are applicable in the southern, just in reverse.

  When the sun is at high noon, it is due north.

- **The Southern Cross.** The Southern Cross is the major navigational constellation of the southern hemisphere. It looks like a tilted cross composed of 4 stars. Whatever its position and whatever time of year, you can follow the long axis from top to bottom in a straight line for about 4½ times the length of the cross to a point in space corresponding to the southern celestial pole. Draw an imaginary line from this "point" straight down to the horizon and you'll have located due south.

Weather

Weather doesn't do much for us in terms of determining direction, but it does mean a great deal in terms of travel, movement, and shelter. You are at the mercy of Mother Nature, and you must respect her temperament and her terms.

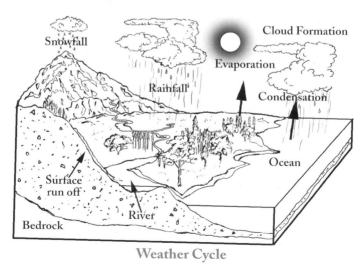

Weather Cycle

My purpose in this section is to give some general weather-prediction tips so you can do a decent job of reading basic weather patterns. Plan your moves accordingly.

There are a few pithy sayings that go a long way toward reading the weather:
Red sky at night, sailor's delight. (This means the sky is dry and it's not likely to rain for a while.)
Red sky in morn, best to warn. (If the light of the sunrise is more red than yellow, expect stormy weather.)
Grey-breaking day, all is ok. (This is the normal morning sky before the sun comes up, and means a normal day.)
Grey at night, wet all right. (This means the clouds are so thick they cover up the setting sun's light. Expect rain.)

What to Look For

Sometimes you can smell moisture in the air, or things sound different, as if you can hear farther. This is the quiet, dead space between the atmospheric pressure waves before a storm comes. Or you can see the smoke from your fire dancing about instead of just trickling upwards. Or you can feel the drop in atmospheric pressure, or change in temperature, or just feel the wind either stop suddenly or pick up rapidly. Other signs of weather to look for include:

- **People.** Some folks get aches and pains in anticipation of wet weather, or their hair curls up with moisture, indicating that rain could be approaching.

- **Animals.** Excessive activity in the middle of the day may be an early warning of bad weather. When animals go all quiet, a storm is imminent.

- **Skies.** A rainbow usually means the storm is past.

If there's enough moisture in the air, you can sometimes see a ring around the sun or moon. If the ring is large or loose, then the moisture is thin and the weather will be ok. If the circle around the sun or moon is tight and small, it means denser moisture in the air, and an increased chance of precipitation. So . . .

The bigger the ring, the better the weather.

Small ring in the sky, you won't be dry.

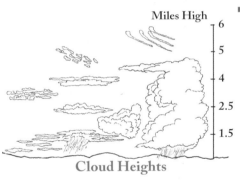

Miles High

6

5

4

2.5

1.5

Cloud Heights

- **Clouds.** Aside from hard and increasing winds, one of the best ways to predict oncoming weather is to look at the clouds. There are many different types, and many varied combinations. The main things to know are that when they're dark, they're full of water. When they're close to the ground, they're ready to dump on you. That said, here's your class on clouds:

The Good: Bright, white, puffy, cottonball-looking clouds.

Rippled, sand dune-type clouds.

High-flying, light, wispy, thin-looking clouds.

Also, ground fog in the morning usually means a sunny day is ahead.

The Bad: Clouds that look like someone stretched out a big cotton ball over the sky, leaving small pockets and slight gaps where the cloud is thinner.

Clouds that look like a solid grey blanket has been unrolled across the sky.

The Ugly: These are those very serious tropical storm-type clouds that move in rapidly, and the sky goes black before it pitches down on you.

Also, when you see any of the above cloud formations with one large, tall, fat, pillar-looking cloud, usually with a flat head at the top, it's pushing a bad rain.

- **Lightning.** If you can see it in the distance, prepare to seek shelter before it gets to you. If you can hear it, best to take shelter right away. Shelter is way back in a cave or at the base of a tree in a large cluster of trees at the lowest point you can find. Stay away from high ground and single trees. In open terrain, lay down flat on the ground or in any small gulley or ravine.

To calculate lightning's distance from you, start counting seconds from the moment you see the flash until you hear the thunder. Then divide that number of seconds by 5. So, if you count 10 seconds between the flash and the boom, divide 10 by 5 to get your distance: 2 miles.

Getting There

Route selection is everything.

When choosing your route, choose the path of least resistance. You will probably be weak and tired and hungry, or maybe even ill or injured.

Try to stay on the high ground. Don't drop down unless you have to, since climbing down and back up will wear you out fast.

Walk the ridgelines as much as possible. That way you

can see both sides of the mountain, and double your chances of spotting water or civilization.

If you have to drop down to lower elevations, try to read the ridges and stay on a path that keeps you as high as possible on the land as you and it descend. Beware of "dead ends" that force you to backtrack and waste energy.

Don't walk in valley bottoms unless you are shielding yourself from the wind or looking for water. In low-lying areas you are more likely to encounter thick brush that can make movement difficult. In these cases, drop low to the ground and try to find a game trail to follow out. Then stay out.

Try to give yourself "handrails" by using terrain features such as rivers and ridgelines to keep you on track in case you get disoriented in thick cover or dark.

Try to avoid traversing swamps and mountain ranges. Better to take more time and go around them, unless you're running out of time and forced to take the risk of not making it at all.

Be aware that on sloping terrain you will inevitably drift downward. Try to offset your elevation loss by walking back up a few meters every "click" or so.

If you find yourself fighting too hard, consider altering your route to an easier path.

Don't dogmatically push to reach a planned destination. Your schedule is arbitrary. It's not worth wearing yourself out.

Incorporate food and water stops and rest and sleep areas into your route.

Estimating Distances

Try to estimate the distance to your destination before you

set out. After a day of traveling, you should try to estimate how far you've come, and compare that to how far you expected to get. The difference can help you adjust your planning to better match your actual performance.

If you have a map, use a straight edge to estimate the distance to where you want to go before you set out. The straight edge can be the compass, a protractor, a ruler, a piece of paper, a piece of string, or any flat object that can be held against the scale in the map's legend and use to measure your route's distance.

Remember that elevation can be deceptive. For example, a 45 degree incline will add about 50 meters for every 1,000 meters, or "click," travelled. A 10-click journey on a steep gradient could add an extra kilometer to your overall distance. This can add up over the course of many miles in mountainous terrain.

A good rule of thumb is to allow 1 extra hour travel time for every 1,000 feet of elevation gain. An 8-mile journey that might take only 2 hours on flat ground will take 3 hours if the path climbs a 1,000-foot hill.

- **Estimating Distance without a Map.** The easiest way is the way you know. Use whatever point of reference you're familiar with. Most folks know that a football field is 100 yards, and a basketball court is about 25 meters long. Use these known quantities to estimate unknown distance.

Keeping Track

- **Pace Count.** This is a technique used by the military for millennia to determine distance traveled. It is vital for helping you know where you are at all times. It is also critical knowledge in planning how far you can expect to go in any given terrain and amount of time.

In its simplest form, pace count is just a matter of counting your steps. For this to have meaning, you need to know how far your step carries you. So we measure.

On a flat surface, like a road, I walk 100 meters at a comfortable speed in 63 paces. If the terrain is uneven, but still fairly flat, like out in the woods, I take 68 paces to make 100 meters. This is an average pace count.

The more difficult the terrain, like thick jungle, or the steeper, the more steps I take, so my pace count increases. If I'm carrying a full rucksack, or moving at night, or sick and tired and hungry, I will take smaller steps, and so again my pace count will increase.

To determine your pace count, measure 100 meters on the most level ground you can find. Use a piece of string measured against your own height, or any other known entity, and tie it at both ends to a stick or stake. Place the start-point stake in the ground and stretch the string to its length. Repeat the process until you've measured out 100 meters. This is your scale.

Starting with both feet together, take two steps. Where your trailing foot steps past the first-step foot and lands on the ground again, that is one pace.

Count each time your trailing foot strikes the ground.

Walk the 100-meter distance at a normal stride. Do this 4 times.

Take the average of these to find your approximate pace count.

For most men, this is about 55-65 paces. For women it is usually 60-70 paces.

Bear in mind that many factors will affect your pace count and only practice and experience helps refine it so you can adjust or "calibrate" on the fly.

Basic Measurements to Know:
1 meter is approximately 3 feet.
100 meters is the distance you'll be measuring with your pace count (approximately 65 paces).
1,000 meters is a kilometer (KM), or one "click." This is 100 meters times 10, or 650 paces.
1.6 KM is 1 mile. (This is good to know if your map scale is in miles.)

- **Pace Cord.** A pace cord is the most common and easiest-to-use strategy. Take a piece of cord or string. Make it about 1 foot long. Tie a knot at the top and a knot at the bottom, and one more about 2/3 of the way up. Then take 9 smaller pieces of string and tie them into knots around the longer segment the cord. Now tie 4 smaller pieces in knots around the shorter segment. Make the knots tight enough to stay put, but loose enough to slide up and down the cord. Now you have a pace cord.

Tie it to your shirt or belt loop. Slide all the knots to the top on each segment. Begin walking and counting your pace. When you get to your 100-meter pace count, slide the bottom knot on the 9-knot segment down to mark 1 100-meter segment walked.

After your second 100-meter pace count, slide down another knot. Keep repeating this. Let's say you get to your destination, a watering hole down the hill from your base camp, and there are 6 knots at the bottom of your pace cord, you have traveled 600 meters.

After 9 knots, you'll mark your tenth 100-meter walk by sliding down the bottom knot of the 4-knot segment. Each of these four knots indicates 1,000 meters, or 1 KM, or 1 click. Rest your 9 knots to the top of the cord's longer segment and begin again.

With this technique, all you need to do is count your 100-meter pace mark of 65 steps or so, and let the cord keep track of the rest.

Some alternatives to the pace cord are to pick up a pebble or break off a piece of twig and put it in your pocket every 100 meters. Once you have 10 of them, just move them from one pocket to another until you've traveled a click. Move them back to the first pocket for the next click, and so on.

- **Tracking Distance with Time.** Sometimes, you may have too much on your mind, or other matters to deal with, to effectively do a pace count. If you have a watch, another— though much less accurate—way to measure distance is to let time doing the counting for you.

It takes a person in decent shape and average health, on average, about 15 minutes to walk 1 mile at a normal pace on a flat road. This means the average person walks about 4 mph. Folks who are older, ill, or not in shape may walk at only 3 mph, meaning they cover a mile in 20 minutes.

If 1.6 KM = 1,600 meters = 1 mile = 20 minutes, then:
400 meters = 5 minutes, and:
100 meters = 1 minute, 15 seconds

Generally speaking, and depending on your rate of speed and specific circumstance, you'll travel about 100 meters every minute or so.

Whatever it takes, remember: Never quit!

8

SIGNALS

Get seen, get heard, get found, get home!

Signals are some of the most important tools in survival. If the rescue didn't start as soon as you went missing, it likely won't start until the survivor sends a signal.

The principles of signaling are pretty straightforward: Make yourself seen and/or heard.

The first thing you want to do in any survival situation is **preparation**! Always let someone know where you are and where you intend to go, when, how, how long, with whom and with what! Leave a written plan when possible, verbal at minimum.

If you have a working radio or a phone, you're probably not truly surviving so much as just tolerating temporary discomfort until help arrives. When you have no means of direct communication and you're stranded, that's a survival situation, and it's in these situations that signaling is so important.

Take an inventory of any resources you have at hand. Some, like a whistle, are good for signaling over short distances, and some, like strobe lights, are better for longer distances. Some signaling tools are one-time use only, like rocket flares, or limited-use, like a beacon with just a few days' worth of battery power left. Simple, low-tech signals like clothes can be laid on the ground to spell "HELP" or "SOS" without too much effort, or you may be able to arrange rocks and branches in similar fashion (if they'll contrast with the background enough to be seen). But only go to the effort if you have the time and energy to gather a bunch of rocks and branches, and if you're sure you plan on staying put for a while. There's little point marking a camp you won't be at unless you have time and energy and resources, like a group of people with extra hands.

Radios

If you have an actual rescue two-way radio, and you can see an aircraft or vessel, be sure to keep the antenna perpendicular or "broadside" to the target instead of pointing it at the vessel you're trying to signal. The strongest signal radiates out from the length of the antenna, not at the tip. This applies to any sort of antenna you might rig up.

It's also good to know that most radios and beacons have only about 72 hours' worth of power, so use them wisely. But also know that all aircraft and sea vessels monitor the distress channels, and if you don't think you'll survive for 72 hours, it might behoove you to just turn it on and leave it on and hope for a speedy rescue.

Here are some good general rules to follow when implementing any communication plan, especially when the power supply, whether batteries or engine fuel, is a finite resource:

- **Where.** Always broadcast from the highest, most open, and most likely to be spotted vantage point, where visual signals can be seen from the greatest distance, and broadcast transmissions travel farthest.

- **When.** Try to concentrate your power-based communications in the first 24 hours, as this is when most search parties will be initiated. Broadcast your signal continuously during this window if you're able.

Consider delaying your 24-hour broadcast period for a day or two if you have reason to believe it will take folks that long to begin looking for you.

After the initial broadcast period, you'll need to go into power-conservation mode. This means spacing out the broadcasts and standardizing their length.

Transmit at dawn, dusk, noon, and midnight. Dawn and dusk are when atmospheric changes can help broadcasts travel enormous distances. At midnight the sky is "stable," as it is at noon. These will be your standard broadcasting times. Transmit from 5 minutes before until 5 minutes after the hour and the half hour. Most radio broadcasts begin at the "top" or "bottom" of the hour, so that's when most people start tuning in their frequency. If you do have a radio, tune to one of the big channels, like 5.000, 10.000, 20.000, etc., as these are used to broadcast WWV universal coordinated time, and people all over the world use this to set their watches.

And remember, it's illegal to broadcast without a license, but if you're trying to get rescued, just dare the authorities to come arrest you!

Lights

Radio contact isn't the only way to call for help.

Any light, even a pocket penlight, can save you in a survival situation.

- **Flash Light.** The standard handheld flashlight can typically be seen at a range of approximately 5 miles, depending on weather and terrain.

- **Strobe Light.** The individual-sized strobes found in many survival kits can be seen for about 10 miles on a clear night, and perhaps as many as 20.

- **Vehicle/Aircraft/Watercraft Lights.** These can be seen for 5 to 15 miles over open terrain under various weather conditions. Note: Even if the weather is foul, if SAR crews know you are out there, they will continue to look, provided the weather is not so bad as to put their vessels and lives at risk. Don't give up hope just because the weather is bad—rescuers might still be looking, and they may still be able to find you. If the weather is extremely dangerous, best to save your lights and settle in to ride out the storm.

- **Laser Pointers.** These are often overlooked as a means of signaling, but they have very good range.

- **Chemlights.** Also known as glow-sticks (or **cyalume** lights), these have a range of about 5 miles, and are very effective when tied to the end of a string and swung around in circles.

- **Homemade Lanterns.** Find some cups, tin cans, or chunks of sandstone, clay, chalk or other soft stone that can be hollowed out to contain animal fat or engine oil or any other liquid fuel. Use a piece of twine or cloth cord, or even pith from a fibrous plant, as a wick, soaking it in the oil until it's fully saturated. Position the wick so it hangs partway out of the container while staying in contact with the liquid fuel. Light the wick and you've got a lantern. When protected from the wind and arranged in a triangle, three lanterns can make a very effective SOS signal.

- **Fire.** This is the most likely resource for the survivor in most situations. If fuel is scarce, fire's use for cooking and warmth must be weighed against its potential use as an emergency signal. Likewise, if your resources for starting a fire are limited, you'll have to make a decision whether to use them now or later.

Build signal fire on a platform to elevate it

Set fire to a dead tree or a living pine tree that stands on its own

Fire Signals

Smoke & Mirrors and Other Signals

Many other visual signals are available to you, some obvious, some not so obvious, and all should be used at every opportunity and in whatever ways time and resources permit. There is virtually no limit to what you can use to signal for help.

- **Smoke.** Light is only one aspect of a fire that can be seen at great distances. Don't neglect smoke as part of your signaling plan. Green leaves and green plants are excellent for generating white smoke. Burning rubber creates a thick, black smoke. Again, be careful to stay upwind, as inhalation can cause sickness.

- **Mirrors.** The military estimates the effective signaling range of a mirror at 50 to 100 miles. On a sunny day, metal can reflect sunlight as far as 10 miles.

- **Space Blankets.** These shiny silver blankets can be torn or cut into strips and tied or staked out to blow in the wind.

- **Clothes.** Clothing that's bright, white, or shiny is best, and can be spread out on the ground to spell HELP or SOS.

Morse Code

Morse code is an old-school but effective way to communicate that you can use with almost any means of communication: light, mirrors, whistles, even fires.

Morse code is also the only signal that will transmit through a nuclear-charged environment when the airwaves are full of static and charged particles, Morse code can still be heard because it is simply a pattern in the otherwise steady static background.

Even a broken radio or phone can transmit sparks of static that can be controlled to send Morse code.

The Morse Code

A .-	H	O —-	V ...-	1 .—	6 -....
B -...	I ..	P .—.	W .—	2 ..—	7 —...
C -.-.	J .—	Q —.-	X -..-	3 ...—	8 —..
D -..	K -.-	R .-.	Y -.—	4 ....-	9 —.
E .	L .-..	S ...	Z —..	5	0 ——
F ..-.	M —	T -			
G —.	N -.	U ..-			

Keep in Mind

- **The Rule of Threes.** There are 3 dots and 3 dashes in the 3-letter Morse code for SOS. That's no accident. The universal distress signal is anything in threes.

Changes in the Air

The new system of some half-dozen satellites specifically dedicated to search and rescue, circle the globe every 100 minutes or so, like the National Oceanic and Atmospheric Agency's SARSAT.

Note: In 2007 the U.S. Coast Guard made the new frequency 406 MHz for any devices transmitting for SAR. But satellites have limitations as well. Most cover only about 60% of the earth's surface, so there are "dead" spots. So keep the fires burning and never quit!

9

FIRST AID

Before we get started on medicine, you should understand that everyone gets ill and injured as a part of life. Keep this in mind when you get hurt or sick so that you do not despair or spiral downward. You will probably get ill or injured, maybe multiple times, before you get out or rescued. Do everything you can to prevent it. But should it happen, learn from it so you don't repeat your mistakes.

In this chapter, I will share my years of training, education, experience and practice to give you every chance at survival. And I'll tell you right now, it can get real ugly. Use this knowledge wisely because it's your own life or that of loved ones you'll save.

Ground Rules

While much of this is actually proper medicine, recognized as such by authorities as acceptable practices, some of what you'll learn is just plain extreme medicine that no one could recommend or do unless faced with dying or watching someone else die.

Anatomy & Physiology

The human body can be seen much like a car, with a series of systems that cooperate to make the machine work. A fault in one system may show up as an improper response in another system, but usually, an electrical issue shows up as an electrical issue and an engine issue as an engine issue.

Basic Systems and Symptoms
Integumentary (skin): Watch for rashes and infections.
Musculoskeletal (muscle & bone): They don't work, you don't work.
Respiratory (breathing): If this stops, it's game over.
Circulatory (blood): Got a leak? Plug it fast!
Digestive (food): Sometimes things get blocked up, or won't stop flowing.
Genitourinary (water & sex): Dehydration is the main problem.
Nervous (brain & pain): Headaches and injuries.
EENT (eye, ear, nose & throat): Something going awry with the senses.
Endocrine (hormones): Outside the scope of survival medicine.

■ **Fever.** This is the human body's number one "engine" light, if you will. When something is wrong, the human body tries to fix it. And, whether ill or injured, white blood cells get mass produced and go to work. As they do, their increase in the blood stream increases body temperature. This is a simple explanation so don't get hung up on it. The key thing is this: **fever is a symptom**, not a cause. Still, it needs to be controlled because it reduces the body's overall function. So, cool down your patient, give him aspirin or try some of the other techniques we'll discuss. Do not let a fever rage out of control. A fever above 106 degrees can damage brain cells or cause death. Be on the alert for black urine, which is a sure sign that the brain is cooking and your patient needs to be cooled down!

■ **Vital Signs.** In general, most folks have the same vital signs. Below are the normal ranges. More fit people tend to have them just a bit lower, and less fit folks a bit higher.

■ **T—Temperature:** 98.6 degrees Fahrenheit (37 degrees Celsius) is typical, but normal temperature may vary one degree F in either direction.

Without a thermometer, body temperature is hard to estimate. Begin by factoring in the ambient temperature and feeling your own head as a baseline. If the patient is conscious, ask if he feels fevered. If you are sick, try to record what you observe when you're with it enough to write.

The basic ranges of temperature are broken down into groups of three degrees:

98-100 degrees F (37-38 degrees C) is a low-grade fever. Usually, the body will handle it fine.

101-103 degrees F (38-39 degrees C) is a mid-grade fever. Control the temperature with aspirin and consider employing antibiotics if they are available.

104-106 degrees F (40-41 degrees C) is a high-grade fever. Keep cool at all costs. Try submerging in cold water or placing cold, wet cloths under armpits, on neck, on groin and behind knees. Strip naked.

■ **P—Pulse:** The pressure we feel on arteries close to the surface of the skin tells us how fast the heart is beating.

This is important to measure and anyone can measure it by feeling the neck, the wrist, the ankle or anywhere arteries are close to the surface. The average pulse is 60-100 beats per minute (BPM). Fit people might have a pulse up to 10 BPM lower than typical and unfit folks could have one as much as 20 BPM higher. Pulse may also be affected by running, working or worrying.

Take someone's pulse by placing two fingers on an artery and using your watch to time the beat. **Do not use your thumb; it has an artery and you'll only measure your own pulse!** You only need to count the beats or "pulses" for 15 seconds. Multiply what you count by four to get one-minute pulse. For example, if you count 20 pulses in 15 seconds, the person has a pulse of 80 – Normal!

Note: In trauma or illness, there is usually an increase in pulse and breathing during the early stages. In the late stages, both of these can slow down below normal.

- **R—Respiration:** The amount of times a person takes a breath in one minute is his respiration rate. On average, this is 16-20 breaths per minute, which translates into 4-5 breaths in a 15-second period. Trauma, pain, working and running will cause increased breathing rate.

- **B/P—Blood Pressure:** Another important vital sign is blood pressure. It is difficult to measure without the right tools, however it is an important assessment tool, especially when there is traumatic blood loss.

B/P is measured in two ranges. The top range (*systolic*) is the higher pressure caused when the heart contracts and pushes blood through the system. The bottom range (*diastolic*) is the pressure that stays in the system, even when the heart is relaxed or dilated. Systolic blood pressure ranges from 100 to 140, averaging about 120. Diastolic blood pressure ranges from 60 to 100, averaging about 80.

The main reason these ranges are important is they allow you to understand what's typical and how to assess a patient's blood pressure in the field, when there is significant blood loss. Gauging this will tell you a lot about how bad off a patient is, and what survival measures you need to consider. Check these with 2 fingers to assess:

Behind the ankle bone = B/P about 90 systolic; still low but far enough from the heart to be good news

Femoral pulse (groin area) = B/P about 80 systolic

Wrist = B/P about 70 systolic

Neck (side of windpipe) = B/P at least 60 systolic; worst-case scenario

Triage

Basically, there are four categories for triage, which you can remember with the acronym D-E-A-D (although the technical terms are in parentheses):

- **Dead or Dying (Expectant)**—These patients will die no matter what. Also, patients in this category could be people who would require so much effort to save that others who could recover might otherwise die. Do not attempt to save the hopeless, like someone who is chopped in half but still alive. Leave them be and attend to others.

- **"E"mmediate (Immediate)**—These are patients who will absolutely die without help but absolutely can be helped. For example, a quick tourniquet can save the life of someone with a leg amputated at the thigh. Without it, he'll be dead in one minute. Deal with immediate cases on discovery.

- **ASAP (Urgent)**—These patients have serious wounds and require treatment soon but could survive for up to 60 minutes without treatment. A typical instance of this triage level includes a gut wound with some guts hanging out but no massive bleeding. Another example would be someone with some fingers chopped off. It's bad news but no one is going to bleed to death from that. Get to it as soon as you can.

- **Delayed (Minimal)**—These injuries range from a broken forearm to an eye hanging out or a good cut. The patients can make it up to six hours without attention and still be okay. **Address these cases at your first chance but understand that they can wait.**

Levels of Pain

There's a fifth vital sign you'll need to gauge in addition to temperature, pulse, respiration and blood pressure if you want to understand your patient's condition: pain. It's classified as follows:

- **Alert**—If you can hear a person yelling and screaming, he's okay for the moment. The noise means he's conscious, breathing, awake and talking. It's a good sign that his body is stable enough that all systems are still functioning.

- **Verbal**—When someone clearly traumatized stops yelling but still responds when spoken to, even if it's only a groan, things have actually gotten a bit worse. Still, a reply shows he's still hearing and processing what's going on. Not so bad, yet. . .

- **Pain**—When a patient is no longer chattin' atcha, you will have to resort to more extreme measures to get his attention and figure out how much pain he's suffering. One way to do this is a sternal rub, rubbing your knuckles hard on the sternum (the hard flat bone in the middle of your chest) to elicit a response. (It hurts like heck. Try it on yourself.) The patient should shudder or groan in response, even if he's unconscious. If the sternal rub doesn't work, try plucking him in the eye with your finger to see if he twitches or blinks. Any response means your patient is still functioning at some level. If there is no response at all, that ain't so good.

- **Unconscious**—The lowest category of being in touch with reality, unconsciousness means your patient shows some kind of vital signs of life but isn't responsive at all.

　　Remember this—the operator feels no pain. Pain is the patient's problem because pain is not a cause; it is only a symptom.

Types of Pain

The sensation of pain as experienced by your patients will help you understand which systems are damaged. There are a number of ways to categorize pain and a few different theories used in the field of medicine. What's important for you in the field is that pain can tell you about what you can't see or measure any other way if you classify it this way:

- **Throbbing pain** usually indicates that something is restricting blood flow, maybe swelling from a bite or a fracture. Move the fracture just a little to allow the blood to flow better and stop the throbbing. Try to reduce the swelling by elevating the limb, loosening a dressing that might be too tightly applied or applying cold or hot compresses on the affected area.

- **Electric impulses and tingling** usually indicates an issue with a nerve. A slipped disk in the spine or a pinched nerve in a fracture is the usual suspect. Do what you can, but treatment is very limited without pain control medications. This type of pain sometimes feels like fire and is sensitive to hot and cold.

- **Dull, constant pain** is usually found with musculoskeletal injuries like sprains, fractures and strains of bones, tendons, ligaments and joints.

- **Sharp pain** usually indicates actual damage to something and is the type of pain felt in most traumatic events where *lacerations* (cuts) occur.

- **Colicky or spasmodic pain** is usually felt when something is wrong with an organ or large muscle mass. The cause could be a lack of oxygen due to decreased blood flow, which in turn could be caused by either swelling from a hard impact or loss of blood from hemorrhaging. Not much can be done in the field for organ damage other than to make the patient comfortable by treating signs and symptoms while offering rest, food, water and time to recover…or not.

TRAUMA MEDICINE

First and foremost is **Scene safety:** make sure it is safe for you first!

C-Spine

The cervical spine has to be on your mind before everything else. Controlling the c-spine is usually not important in survival unless there was a crash.

ABCs of methodological checking

A is for Airway.

Traditionally, clearing the airway is considered the starting point for medical care. **Airway is not the starting point for care in survival medicine. If there is trauma, circulation is the number-one priority. Stop the bleeding first and foremost** because massive bleeding can kill a patient in one minute. If someone is not breathing, he can last a couple of minutes without oxygen—and you can supply air to your patient but not blood.

> ### If the patient doesn't respond to hailing, check these things:
>
> If he's unconscious, make sure he's breathing and turn his head to the side to keep him from choking on his own tongue.
>
> If he's unconscious and not breathing, check his pulse because he might be dead already. If there's no pulse, he's dead. Consider CPR if no one else needs help.
>
> If there is a pulse but no breathing, your patient might need CPR. Before beginning CPR, open his mouth and make sure nothing is blocking the airway. If the airway is blocked, stick your finger in and try and sweep it out. Be careful not to get bit by his gag reflex or push any obstruction deeper.
>
> If there is a pulse but no breathing and no obstructions, give two quick breaths.

That procedure will cover checking the airway. **Very rarely in survival will the airway will be obstructed except for poison, choking or anaphylaxis.**

If your patient's entire face is destroyed and there is nothing but a bloody mess and he can't seem to breathe through it all, consider making a hole in his neck, with a cricothyroidectomy (detailed later).

B is for Breathing.

Checking the airway means just making sure the passage way is open; breathing is making sure the patient is actually sucking air in and out. Checking for a sucking chest wound will tell you. For the survivor's purposes, any hole in the chest sucks. There are two kinds, though, with two different actions required.

- **Pneumothorax (Collapsed Lung).** When you have a hole in your chest, it's easier for the air to come in through the hole than through the pipes of the throat. So, every time the chest rises mechanically when you try to breathe, air rushes into the chest cavity through the hole rather than through the windpipe. That air then gets trapped inside the chest instead of blowing back out because the tissue around the wound seals in expiring air and keeps the air inside the chest.

The more air in the chest, the smaller the lungs get until they can't hold enough air to oxygenate the blood. You must get the air out of his chest.

The treatment is to cover the wound with your hand— or with your patient's hand if he's conscious. Find something waterproof like plastic and cover the wound with that.

It might be necessary to "burp" this wound every once in a while, maybe every five to 60 minutes depending on its severity. If the patient is conscious, he can do it when he feels pressure building up by sticking a finger into the hole, letting the air out to relieve the pressure and then covering the wound back up.

If there is only a small puncture into the chest but the same symptoms are present, you won't be able to burp it with your finger. If you have a medical needle with a hole in the center, stick it into the wound to drain the air. You can also try forcing your finger in or, in the worst-case scenario, cut with a small knife to make the hole big enough to drain air. Only incise enough to widen the hole and drain the air. There will be small amounts of blood but failure to drain the air will result in death.

- **Hemothorax.** If there is an injury to the chest and no air is sucking in and out but breathing is getting increasingly difficult, then chances are your patient is suffering from a hemothorax or blood in the chest. The effects are the same as a pneumothorax, as blood fills the cavity around the lungs.

  Do not drain this blood. The blood will only fill up so much space and will then cause enough pressure to *tamponade* or stop itself from bleeding. In this case, you cover the wound and do not "burp" it. You lay the person on their injured side so that some pressure on the bleeding can help to stop it. If your patient does not lose too much blood into the chest, he may survive, but this too, will require surgery.

Just remember these:

Pneumothorax (air-lung) = injury up, air rises

Hemothorax (blood-lung) = injury down, blood sinks

Tell the difference if you're not sure by auscultating. Do this by tapping on the chest to hear what sounds it makes. If their chest is filling with air it will sound "hyper-hollow" and if it is filling with blood, it will sound "hyper-dull."

C is for Circulation.

For the survivor, it's really easy. Circulation means blood, so stop the bleeding!

Different Types of Bleeding:
Desanguination is loss of major amount of blood, like if two legs get ripped off.
Arterial blood is the bright-red spurting kind that squirts out with every heartbeat like if a forearm were severed off completely.
Venous blood is the dark, oozing kind; while it might be copious, it's rarely fatal.
Minor bleeding is what you might see from a small cut or laceration.

The type of bleeding must be taken into account with the location of the bleeding to have a better picture of the situation and what kind of treatment is warranted.

Major arterial bleeding from an amputated leg can be controlled with a tourniquet in seconds, but major bleeding from a ruptured spleen or torn aorta will cause enough internal bleeding in a minute to cause death without one drop of blood being shed.

Most venous bleeding from say, a seriously excoriated, or scraped-up, chest from a slide down some steep cliff will hurt but will clot fairly soon on its own. A venous bleed on the scalp could cause a person to lose enough blood that they go into shock and die because the scalp is so vascular that it just keeps bleeding.

Rarely will a minor bleed be an issue unless it involves an internal organ or two and the person is slowly bleeding out and becoming anemic and weak over a period of time.

In a survival situation, this could cause death in just a matter of days.

So, the **type** of bleeding and the **location** are the two major factors for considering what the final outcome might be, but the treatment is always the same: **Stop the bleeding!**

It's easy to do. **Just slap your hand directly on the wound and push down.** If your patient is conscious and coherent, make him do it while you find or improvise a dressing. **In case of an amputation, go straight to the tourniquet. If blood is spurting, reach in and pinch it off. If there are two or three spurters, place your knee on one!** Get aggressive, go after the source of that bleeder and stop it ASAP. If you have to stick your finger into an open gut wound and pinch a piece of intestine to stop it bleeding, do so! It's that easy.

The Sequence for Hemorrhage Control:

- **Direct pressure.** The first thing to do is put your hands on the wound or a dressing covering the wound.

- **More pressure.** Add a dressing if there is none or add a second dressing and pack it into the wound more by tying the dressing down with the knot on top of the wound to create more pressure in an attempt to stop the bleeding.

- **Elevation.** Raise the wound above the level of the heart to decrease the blood flow by reducing the amount of pressure on the hole in the circulatory system. This is particularly useful for a bleeding arm or leg if the person is sitting. If you can't get the limb above the heart, get the heart below the limb by laying the person down then raising his arm or leg.

- **Pressure points.** On some locations on the human body, blood vessels are closer to the surface and, as such, pressing down at these points will reduce the blood flow through the vessels to the wound.

- **Tourniquets** are considered a **last resort** in modern medicine. However, recent combat medicine has changed this to the point that a good tourniquet, quickly and correctly applied, is often the first choice for any significant bleeding. This tourniquet will staunch the blood loss and provide the caregiver more time to get the right dressings ready to apply. After the dressing is applied, the tourniquet can be eased up gently, striking a balance during the transition. Also, you can re-tighten a tourniquet while adjusting a dressing. Finally, once the dressing is in place and the bleeding is under control, the tourniquet can be removed completely.

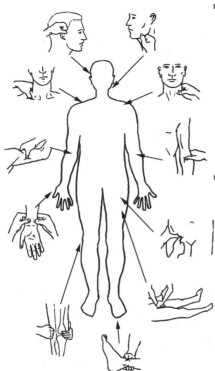

Blood Pressure Points

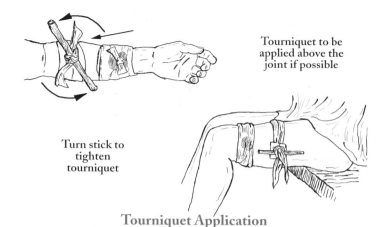

Tourniquet to be applied above the joint if possible

Turn stick to tighten tourniquet

Tourniquet Application

Rules for Tourniquet Usage:

Tourniquets should be two inches wide or wider but not narrower unless nothing wider is available.

Tourniquets should be placed two inches above the wound or amputation. Placing lower could damage the wound.

Placing higher could mean that, if the tissue below the tourniquet dies from lack of blood, the patient will lose more tissue than necessary.

Tourniquets should be tightened only enough to stop the major bleeding; some oozing is okay.

Tourniquets should not be loosened until you have a proper dressing in place and ready.

Tourniquets should be kept ready to be tightened or re-applied if the bleeding begins again.

Tourniquets should be placed **below joints** when possible. If the patient loses his limb later due to amputation, the joint is important to having a better prosthetic.

HYGIENE

Try to maintain your personal hygiene and general cleanliness as a top preventive strategy. This will also help with your sense of general well-being and positive mental outlook. But it also decreases diseases by reducing the bacteria that grow naturally on the human skin and multiply quickly in dirty conditions.

Hygiene Tips:

- **The sun** kills bacteria. If you have no water, try to take off your clothes and expose your skin to the sun for a while, being mindful not to get sunburned.

- **The air** itself can still help kill some bacteria if there is no sun. Just airing out your body for a little while each day, or a few times a day if needed and plausible, can reduce the amount of bacteria on your body.

- **Sand** can be used when there is no water, especially in the armpits and groin. Be careful to get it all out of the butt cheeks to prevent chafing and a rash.

- **Shower** in the rain if you get the chance or use some snow if practical.

- **Teeth** are vitally important in life and become even more so in a survival situation as dental problems can cause misery and grief unlike any other. So, keep your teeth as clean as possible.

- **Feet** are the most important thing for any survivor. Take care of them! Massage them every single day before you start your day and every single night before you end it.

Keep them dry at all cost. If you can't keep them dry, stop a lot and air them out so they dry. No matter how cold it is, air them out. No matter how wet it is, take them out of your boots, even in a downpour of rain, and air them out. Try to rotate socks and keep them clean or get rid of the socks altogether.

Nutrition

When you are surviving, basically, you need to think "caveman diet," 'cause that's pretty much what you're gonna be on. This is mainly meat and some fruits and veggies if you're lucky.

- **Protein** is the number-one thing that is going to give you strength and you are going to need it. The best source of protein is meat from killing animals or catching insects.

- **Fats** are one of the best sources for energy there is. Eat as much as you can.

- **Carbohydrates** are important for energy so eat them when you can from many roots and plants like cattails. (See the Food section for this.)

- **Vitamins & Minerals** fall into the same category for the survivor. You're not likely to get all you need and you don't need that many initially. The lack of them will cause you major problems over a long period of time.

  The chart on the next page explains why.

Vitamin-Deficiency Diseases to Look Out For

Vitamin	Sources	Deficiency	Symptoms
A "Retinol"	Liver, eggs, carrots, many fruits and veggies	Night Blindness	Self-explanatory
B1 Thiamine	Liver, eggs, pork, peas, oranges, potatoes	Beri-beri	Weight loss, emotional disturbances, weakness, pain in limbs, and edema or swelling
B2 Riboflavin	Meat, eggs, fish, milk, bananas, okra, few veggies	Ariboflavinosis	Swelling and redness of mouth and throat, cracking at corners of mouth, pseudo-syphilis or scaling on genitals
B3 Niacin	Meats, eggs, fish, nuts, seeds, beans, lots of veggies, liver, heart, kidney	Pellagra	Aggression, insomnia, sensitivity to sunlight, weakness, mental confusion, skin lesions, dermatitis and hair loss, swollen oral cavity, diarrhea, dementia, limb paralysis, death
B5 Pantothenic Acid	Meats, some veggies	Paresthesia	Pins and needles feeling on the skin without being caused by sleeping on a limb

Vitamin	Sources	Deficiency	Symptoms
B6 Pyridoxine	Meats, nuts, some vegetables	Anemia	Often overlooked, feeling tired, weak, generally aching, irregular breathing and heart beat, pale skin and nail bed, cracks at corner of mouth, and pica, the craving of unusual things to eat
B7 Biotin	Milk, liver, eggs	Dermatitis	Any condition of inflamed skin such as a rash, eczema
B9 Folic Acid	Greens, beans, seeds	Birth Defects	Not a major issue for most survivors
B12 Cyanocobalimin	Meat, shellfish, eggs, milk, termites	Anemia	Same as B6 above
C Ascorbic Acid	Fruits, roses, pine needles, tomatoes	Scurvy	Dark purple spots on skin, bleeding from nose and gums, tooth loss, sunken eyes, opening of old scars and broken bones
D Ergo or Chole-Calciferols	Dairy, sunlight, fatty-type fish	Rickets & Osteomalacia	Weak muscles, painful cramps, easy bone fracturing
E Tocopherols	Nuts, seeds and darker greens	Rare	Hemolytic anemia in newborns
K Mena or Phylloquinines	Darker greens, meats, eggs	Bleeding diathesis	Blood fails to clot

- **Minerals** are in the same category for the survivor as vitamins. You'll get what you get and there are no real significant diseases caused by mineral shortages.

  The only two Vitamins not really provided by meat are Vitamin E, which has no real known deficiency disease and Vitamin C, which is one of the most widely occurring and easy to find vitamin sources almost everywhere in the world! Seaweed at sea, cacti in the desert, lichen in the Arctic, and many plants in the jungle, mountain and forests can provide Vitamin C. With meat and one plant from each of the world's environments, you can survive with a fundamentally healthy diet!

- **Fiber** is almost purely a nicety. Enough fruits, veggies and water will usually suffice.

Immunization

Immunizations are very important. Get the necessary precautionary injections before you go. Prevention is key!

Basic Immunizations Most People Should Get			
Name	**Frequency**	**Prevents**	**Notes**
Meningococcal	Maybe a booster every 5 years or when travelling to endemic area	Brain disease	Can kill you quickly!
Hepatitis A	Lifetime vaccines require multiple doses	Hep A, mostly from water in poor countries	Hep A hurts a lot, but most survive

Name	Frequency	Prevents	Notes
Hepatitis B	Series with boosters	For health-care workers who deal with blood	This does kill
Pneumococcal	A booster every 5 years or if traveling	Lung diseases	Can kill too
Influenza	Annually	Flu	Mostly for elderly and young
Varicella	Usually once	Chickenpox	A herpes virus
HiB (Haemophilus Influenzae)	Maybe 5 years or when travelling to a risky area	Bacterial infections of brain, heart, lungs	Can be lethal
MMR (Measles, Mumps, Rubella)	Might need for travel	Stops what it says on the label	Helps fight other virals
HPV (Human Papilovirus)	3-part series over 6 months, once in life	Disease that is difficult to detect	For sexually active women under 26
TDP (Tetanus, Diphtheria, Pertussis)	Booster every 10 yrs	Prevents Tetanus, which can kill quickly	Usually caused by infected wounds

Note: Check your shot records. Get them up to date!

Disease

Simply put, diseases are a reaction of the human body to naturally occurring organisms which causes a negative impact on the health. They come from many sources, cause many symptoms, and not all have cures. Some go away on their own, some are easily treated, and some are fatal if untreated.

Most diseases can be either treated or cured. Treatment means the disease can be managed to make it less harmful but not killed completely. Curing means the disease can be completely removed as a problem.

Since most things can be cured, or at least treated, the key will be lasting long enough to get treatment or a cure. To this end, it is helpful to know what diseases are out there and what causes them so you can try to **prevent** them when possible while recognizing signs and symptoms if you do get something. This way, you can understand what is going on if you get sick, try to keep any sickness from getting worse, have some idea what to expect so you don't despair, and have a concept of the timeline you are up against to help make better decisions to effect a rescue or escape to civilization.

I will include treatments just in case you happen to have medical supplies. How to use them will depend on more variables than I can cover here. Read the label; then use your common sense and best SWAG (scientific wild-ass guess!).

Diseases to Look Out For

Disease	Vector/Cause	Signs/Symptoms	Treatment
Malaria Protozoan Parasites	Mosquito (dawn/dusk biter) Tropics	Fever in cycles, chills, jaundice, sweats	Chloroquine and other options
Leish-maniasis Protozoan	Sandfly Africa, Asia, Mediter-ranean	Cutaneous: Skin ulcers, fever. Visceral: Liver and spleen enlarge	Fatal if not treated. Antimony, Amphotericin, Miltefosine
Leptospirosis (spirochete bacteria)	Rat urine but many animals can carry and cause it	High fever, bad aches, chills, headaches, then brain, liver and kidney damage leading to death; brown urine is a bad sign	Doxycycline, Penicillin, Ampicillin, Amoxicillin
Histo-plamosis (fungal infection of the lungs)	Bat & bird feces, usually from being in caves or near cliffs with birds	Harsh coughing for no apparent reason two weeks after being around bat or bird droppings	Amphotericin-B or other Systemic anti-fungals. Consider Diflucan. Unexplained dark lesion around nose and mouth is indicator
Scabies	Mites from poor hygiene, primarily bedding	Itchiness and red skin and rash as mite burrows into flesh and lays eggs	Permethrin Lindane Ivermectin

Disease	Vector/Cause	Signs/Symptoms	Treatment
West Nile virus	Mosquito bite with robins and crows making virus worse	Fever with chills, sweats and swollen lymph nodes	No treatment. Consider antivirals
Rickettsia causes Typhus, Pox and Rocky Mountain spotted fever	Ticks, fleas, lice usually off of rats, causes some types of encephalitis, too	Fevers, chills, aches, nausea, vomiting; there are vaccines	Bacteria is gram negative and responds well to antibiotics, looks a lot like dengue
Filariasis or Elephantiasis Nematode Worm	Mosquito bite carries worm, gets into lymph system	Skin thickens like an elephant's, mostly lower legs; can affect anywhere	Diethylcarbamazine Albendazole Doxycycline
Onchocerciasis or River blindness; Nematode Worm related to above	Parasite in black fly bite near flowing rivers	Gets in body, causes severe itching, then thick lizard skin; migrates to eyes, causes opaqueness and blindness	Ivermectin Doxycycline
Dengue	Mosquito (day biter) Asia, Africa, Caribbean, Latin America, Australia	Rash on lower legs and chest, high fever, abdominal pain, constant headaches, loss of appetite	Goes away on its own, but if there is hemorrhage do not give aspirin, which will reduce clotting

Disease	Vector/Cause	Signs/Symptoms	Treatment
Sleeping Sickness (Trypanosomiasis)	Tsetse Fly, Africa Attracted to dark clothes and fast moving objects	Fever, headaches, joint pain, swollen lymph nodes, daytime sleepiness; fatal if untreated	Eflornithine, Pentamidine
Chagas Disease or American version of Trypanomiasis	Assassin or kissing bug bites Latin America	Causes a nodule at bite site, then disease spreads for up to 20 years	Drugs from Azole family—Benznidazole, etc. but only early on, hard to treat later
Yellow Fever	City or rainforest mosquito Central & South America	Fever, chills, and bleeding into skin Hits in two to three days with jaundice, coffee-ground-looking vomit, goes away after jaundice, then comes back and often kills	Vaccine is 99% effective No treatment, only for symptoms
Bilharzia or **Schistosomiasis** (Trematodes)	Parasite from snail in fresh water called flukes	Rash and itchy skin one to two days after wading in water, then fever and aches	Praziquantel, Antimony

Note: The type of parasite is listed not to be fancy, but to help you as a survivor and improviser extraordinaire. In case you come across a medication for one type you might use it for another of the same type. For example, you might find the anti-helminthic, Praziquantel, which is used to treat Trematodes also called Flukes. But you might actually have a flatworm, also called tape worm, from the Cestode family. The Praziquantil can be used for both even though the second is an "off-label" use, meaning the parasite is not the medication's intended target. Still, it can still kill that other parasite because they are similar. Use what you have and think outside the box.

Antibiotic Therapies for the Survivor

- **Rules.** There are a lot of rules and laws regarding antibiotics. These are good because, if antibiotics were readily available to everyone, many folks would wrongly take them, develop an immunity and then they would be less effective later when they need them.

- **Exceptions to the Rules.** The survivor has but one mission, to stay alive. Illness can cause this mission to fail. So, antibiotics are to be considered fully acceptable for use in a survival situation. That said, you need to know some basics about bugs and drugs.

- **Two Types.** There are primarily two types of bacteria that have significance to the survivor, the kind that need oxygen and the kind that don't (called *aerobic* and *anaerobic* bacteria, respectively). This is only intended as kindergarten-level class.

Three Terms. The terminology: *gram negative* and *gram positive* and broad spectrum. Theses help docs know what best to use for the aerobic or anaerobic bacteria, like a sniper rifle. The key for the survivor is the *broad spectrum antibiotic*, like a shotgun, it works against both kinds.

■ **Diagnosing.** The types of bacterial infections you might get on a cut on the outside of your arm are usually aerobic and gram positive and less severe. The types you might get inside you, like a deep puncture, where there is no air, are usually anaerobic and gram negative and are usually more severe.

When you attempt to diagnose a bacterial infection in the field without the benefit of tools and lab, it is called *empirical diagnosis*—based purely on experience and observation. Use the info you gather to try and decide what kind of infection is being presented. That will drive the determination of which drug might be needed. In short, it is a best guess.

A good rule of thumb is that green is bacterial, yellow is viral. This is useful for determining if you actually need that antibiotic or not when there is a cough, runny nose or phlegm.

It is important to grasp that not all antibiotics work for all bacterial infections. So if you are taking an antibiotic for something that it is not designed and intended for, it might not be doing you any good at all and you've squandered a valuable resource that could have been of benefit later if used for the bugs it was intended to work against.

What it all means to you is this: incorporate what you now know about the basics of antibiotics and bacteria and make the best guess for what will work based on what you have available to you. In most cases, a broad spectrum antibiotic will work. If in doubt, take the antibiotics.

■ **Treatment.** When it comes right down to it, it is best to have some broad spectrum antibiotics. Try to get them, try to keep them in any first aid/survival kit and if you have them, chances are, they will help. Here is a list of a few; these will change over time so do some research for the most current medicines. I include here one common broad-spectrum antibiotic from each of the major categories so that if you encounter one of these, you will know it can be of good use.

Clindamycin
Ciprofloxacin, Levofloxacin
Doxycycline
Trimethoprim-Sulfamethoxazole
Ceftriaxone
Amoxacillin
Erythromycin, Azithromycin
Kanamycin

Note: Most medications will last much longer than their shelf life. Very rarely is an out-of-date medicine actually more harmful as a result of being expired. Consider the temperature and conditions of storage and time expired, but if the container looks good and the medication looks normal, give it a try.

Diarrhea

There are simple general concepts and rules for dealing with diarrhea:

Let diarrhea go for the first 24 hours to clear out any causative organisms unless you are moving or already ill.

If you are moving or already dehydrated, try to stop it up, ASAP!

If diarrhea lasts more than a day, chances are it is a bug, not just bad food.

Viral diarrhea will be very aggressive, hit hard and fast, and pass in one to three days.

Bacterial diarrhea takes a while to build up and is slower to go away.

When fever, vomiting, blood or pus are present, consider antibiotics.

Antibiotics will not help with viral causes of diarrhea.

In all cases, drink fluids, stay hydrated, treat symptoms and reduce fever.

Here is a chart of some of the causes of diarrhea and how to help you determine what type you might have so you can best determine how to deal with it. It is important to know that the majority of diarrhea is from a bacterial cause.

Causes of and Treatments for Diarrhea

Type or Cause	Major Sign or Symptoms	Primary Treatment
E.Coli (many types)	In survival situations, usually shows up without fever, often from dirty food, poor hygiene	Usually gram negative so use narrow spectrum antibiotics if available or Amoxicillin
Dysentery: oral-fecal **Amoebic:** E.Histolitica **Bacterial:** See below—Shigella, Salmonella, Campylobacter	Can vary but usually are considered to be of the worst types with longest persistence. Fever, blood, pus maybe, but frequent diarrhea after anything is ingested	Primary mission is to keep hydrated with fluids, enemas, IVs. Oral rehydration solutions made with some salt and sugar, etc. Flagyl will treat E.Histolitica and Cipro will treat the three bacterias.
Shigella (gram negative) oral-fecal route means dirty hands after latrine or flies landing on feces then food, causes about ⅓ of cases of diarrhea	Usually with fever, blood, pus in stool, often with cramps, nausea, vomiting and straining to defecate, starts in two days, lasts four days or longer	Ampicillin, Ciprofloxacin
Salmonella (gram negative) found on turtles/reptiles, usually food-borne from food cooked but not eaten right away	Mostly from eggs and poultry, fever with headache and rose spots and diarrhea with blood and mucous	Usually hits a few hours after ingestion, lasts a few days and goes away on its own.

Type or Cause	Major Sign or Symptoms	Primary Treatment
Cholerais (gram negative), causes an enterotoxin which makes it meaner than most	Painless, watery diarrhea, rapid onset usually two days, rarely with vomiting or fever	Fluids, symptomatic, sometimes antibiotics, no vaccine
Giardia Lamblia is a protozoa, no antibiotic will work, usually from drinking bad water, these cysts survive many filters (boil drinking water)	Diarrhea rarely has pus or blood, but often foul-smelling flatulence and eructations or burps, rarely fever	Metronidazole or Flagyl but this is a long course. Tinidazole is a single dose, can go away on its own in a few weeks
Campylobacter, oral-fecal, sexual, contaminated food, water, raw meat	Fever, diarrhea usually without blood, cramps	Mostly goes away on its own
Vibrio P (gram negative)	Usually from brackish water and seafood, watery diarrhea within 24 hours	Mostly goes away on its own
Rotavirus causes a lot of diarrheas from contaminated hands	Usually within two days, can last four to eight days, profuse diarrhea, sometimes vomit, low grade fever	Hydration is imperative, this will go away, but loss of fluids is worse with this since antibiotics will not help
Typhoid Fever is a strain of salmonella	It causes diarrhea without blood, a high-grade fever, rose spots on chest, nose bleeds	Usually not fatal, antibiotics help like Chloramphenicol or Cipro

REAL FIRST AID

CPR—The Real Deal

The fact is that everyone is going to die. Sometimes, in very rare circumstances, this can be reversed by CPR. In some states, the out-of-hospital survival rate for CPR patients is as low as 3%.

This means two very important things to a survivor. First, if you didn't witness someone go down, and find no breathing or pulse, chances are, they will not recover. Second, if you do recover them, be able to sustain them. This could be painful to recover a life, only to watch it slip away again.

Now, I'm not saying not to try CPR. If you're fit and strong, there are no other patients, you're not in danger from the environment and you think you can recover and sustain them, then give it a go.

The main reason for CPR in a survival situation is twofold. The first reason is trying to do something for yourself. If you don't want to accept your patient's death, then get down there and try. The second reason is to help the surviving loved ones. If there is a husband present who just witnessed his wife die, you might try and administer CPR, for him! He'll see that you are trying, and knowing that you did try, he can more easily accept the hard facts. Later, this will help with group cohesion in the survivor dynamics because there is no anger at you for not trying and maybe even a closer bond for having tried.

So, what I am saying is that CPR in a survival situation is mostly for you and the other survivors, not for the dead and dying. It is hard work and will drain you and this must be considered, especially early on in any traumatic crash type scenario.

Exceptions—Lightning & Drowning

Now, for every rule, there are almost always exceptions and this is true for Survivor CPR, too. If you see a fellow survivor get struck by lightning, or have a bad fall, or drown and you rescue them, in these cases, CPR is very effective and can very much stand a chance of bringing someone back to life! **No breathing, but pulse, give two breaths. No pulse or breaths, then do CPR.**

Precordial thump

Basic CPR addressed, consider this great little trick called a *precordial thump*. It is the closest thing to a defibrillator you're gonna get in the field.

Because the heart is like a little electrical battery, sometimes a jumpstart is all you need to get it back to work. And that is what the precordial thump does. Execute it with one good blow, striking with the bottom (palm aspect) of your fist, right on top of the center of the heart. Use a firm blow but pull back so as to not break ribs.

Often, if you witness a case of "heart attack," a precordial thump will kick start the heart. It can save a life and save you a lot of work. It shouldn't be done more than once, or two to three times tops. If it doesn't work then, it ain't gonna work, so get to doing CPR. Good luck with that!

Golden 60, 60, 6

- **Golden Minute.** The first 60 seconds will often dictate a lot about the chances for a patient's survival. If they have a leg chopped off and are bleeding out, chances are, if you don't intervene within that first minute, they will bleed out and die.

    If someone has their face smashed and can't breathe for over a minute, chances are they will suffocate and die.

    The chances of someone surviving without the two critical requirements of blood and air, after more than a minute, are very slim indeed.

- **Golden Hour.** The human response to trauma is a shock response that makes a patient hyperventilate to get more air while his blood vessels constrict to save loss of blood. This passes quickly, however, and then the blood flows and the breathing shallows. During this time is when your treatments will most impact a patient's chance of survival.

- **Golden Six Hours.** After first responder aid and stabilization care is given, your patient will need medical or surgical intervention, depending on the damage done. For the survivor, these first six hours will likely come and go without rescue or aid. Most trauma victims with significant organ and tissue damage will begin to expire without surgical intervention. You must understand this concept and consider these questions:

    To whom do you give limited time, energy and medical supplies?

    Who do you move or not?

    Do you let the person know they are likely not going to make it?

Do you tell their loved ones what the realistic expectations are?

Note: I have found that most of the time, people prefer the truth, so be honest in your assessments to both the dying and the living.

Self-Treatment

- **Dehydration**, a real problem in a survival situation, can cause kidney stones.

  When dehydrated over long periods of time, small pebbles of calcium form in the *ureters* or "tubes" from the kidney to the bladder. There is sudden and severe pain in the flanks with fever. Usually, they will pass. Have the person rest, often on the opposite side, to allow gravity to help move the stone along. Give pain meds and water if available. Try having your patient lie upside down, with their back against a tree and their feet up in the air, and massage the bladder; gravity may dislodge the stone.

- **Diabetes** If their breath smells fruity and they are thirsty and urinating a lot, skin is hot and dry, and breathing is deep and rapid, without insulin, likely, they are going down.

  If your patient needs sugar, the fix is a shot of sugar, but without it, your patient could be in real trouble, too. If he is suddenly hungry, confused, angry, cold and clammy skinned, he is going into insulin shock, meaning too much insulin sucked up his blood sugar.

  If you can't tell which type, giving something sweet won't hurt. If in doubt, whip it out.

- **Poison.** There are only two courses of action available for first-aid responses to poison.

If poison is ingested:
Vomit it out. If you can't do that, or it's been too long…
Try to neutralize the poison internally by consuming charcoal-based fluids.

If the poison comes from contact:
Suction poisons from bites (not with your mouth) and clean the wound.
Clean off the area and treat the symptoms.

Shock

Most people understand allergies. Sometimes, the reaction is mild and sometimes, it's so extreme that without intervention, the body kills itself by over-responding. This is true of **anaphylactic shock**.

Epinephrine or adrenaline injections and diphenhydramine or Benadryl are the two drugs used universally to treat anaphylactic shock. The chances of surviving true anaphylaxis are slim without these.

The other types of shock are not really relevant to the survivor, except for septicemia.

- **Septicemic:** When your patient has a systemic infection, he'll be burning up with fever. Without antibiotics, he will not make it.

Elements & Exposure

Braving the weather is mostly common sense. If it's hot; stay cool. If it's cold; stay warm. If it's wet, get dry. If it's dry, find some wet. But what about when you can't and you start to suffer? Here's what to look for and what you can try to do about it. In severe cases, you might not be able to do anything except take it and drive on, with the hopes of making it out or getting rescued: your only real chance of surviving.

Burns
First-degree burns are the top layer of skin turning red. These hurt but aren't serious.
Second-degree burns go deeper and cause blisters. Later infection is the real danger.
Third-degree burns go past the skin and do not hurt but are the most dangerous.
The treatment is the same for all burns, as follows:
Keep cool and dry.
Use pain medication when needed and available.
If the burn is deep, consider using topical antibiotics.
Burn victims need a lot of fluid, as they will ooze white blood cells and dehydrate.
Do not lance blisters. If you must, lance at the base, not at the top.
If the burn is third-degree, the skin will be grey and painless; the nerves are burnt. These people will need antibiotics because the skin is open and the body exposed to infection.

- **Lightning strikes** can cause burns and are to be treated in the same way depending upon the severity.
- **Heat exhaustion** is merely getting overdone in the sun. Drink lots, stay cool and don't work too hard in the heat. If your skin is cold and clammy, you're still okay, just take it easy as heat exhaustion can quickly lead to heat stroke.

- **Heat stroke** is a flat-out killer. It strikes when the body gets so hot and so dehydrated, that the cooling mechanism of sweating stops. If a person passes out and presents hot and dry skin, he is in a bad way. This is a life threatening emergency. **Cool down by any means.** Without fluids and reduced temperature, someone in this state will expire.

- **Prickly heat** occurs in hot environments, when sweating a lot, the pores will become blocked in the oily parts of skin. This stimulates the tiny nerves on the hair follicles and will be interpreted by the brain as a burning or electrifying sensation. The solution is to wash the area with soap and water.

- **Jungle rot or immersion foot** is when the tissues of the feet disintegrate as a result of being wet too long and then being torn off from too much friction, usually from the boot during walking. The treatment is easy: dry your feet. Take breaks and air them out. Failure to do so will cause infection, gangrene and death.

- **Frostbite** happens when the skin is damaged by cold, rupturing cells and causing blisters. You'll know when you have frostbite because it burns or stings at first. And like third-degree burns, once the body part stops hurting, you're in trouble as it's then frozen. Treat the symptoms just like a burn but remember some important differences about recovering from frostbite.

  Do not thaw things out unless you can keep them thawed. Re-freezing of digits or limbs will worsen their condition and outcome.

  Use the body to get frostbitten parts warm again: feet against stomachs, hands in armpits. Do not use water or fire for re-warming; this must be a gentle process or tissue damage will result.

- **Snow blindness** happens very easily when your eyes experience direct, prolonged exposure to the strong UV rays from bright sunlight reflecting off snow or ice. Protect the eyes when you can with glasses or goggles. Two sticks worn like glasses so you see through the slits or a strip of cloth with a small slit you can see through will also work. In a worst-case scenario, put something dark like shoe polish or mud under your eyes to deflect some of the ultraviolet light.

Commonplace Health Problems

Okay, now that we've covered some serious stuff, let's look at some of the more commonplace, and less life-threatening, health problems a survivor might face.

- **Boils**—an accumulation of pus and dead tissue—occur as hygiene and health deteriorate. Use a warm compress to try and raise the infection closer to the surface then lance the boil with a hot pin and drain the boil from the head.

- **Fungus.** Athlete's foot, crotch rot and ring worm are all fungi that can form anywhere on the body and that are common complaints of survivors. The best treatment in a survival situation is sun, but this will only keep the fungus at bay and will not cure it. Only anti-fungal drugs will remove these.

- **Hemorrhoids** cause a lot of people grief and this can be especially true for the survivor suffering from ailments that cause excess strain on bowel movements. Avoid hemorrhoids by staying hydrated, not forcing defecation and using lubrication.

- **Ticks** are a common problem in the woods. Try not to

burn them off. Use tweezers or string tied around them or even a small toothpick-sized twig to slowly dislodge a tick.

- **Leeches** are the ticks of the jungle and swamp world. The best way is the same was as with the tick. But if needed, burn off or use salt, ash, or tobacco spit.

- **Bugs in ears.** The best way to get rid of bugs when they're diggin' into your ear canal is oil, any type, as this will drown it, then drain it out.

Sprains & Strains

Sprains and strains are typical injuries for survivors. These are often confused.

- **Muscles experience strains** if you lift too much and the muscle tears or tendons stretch from hyperextension. There is a lot of pain in the muscle group.

- **Ligament strains.** Ligaments connect bones to bones, holding the skeleton together. Sprains often happen to ankles when people are running and step on something that causes the weight of the body to force the ankle into an over-extended position.

There are three types of sprain. Here's what they mean to you as a survivor:
If you twist an ankle, but don't fall, it is a Type 1 sprain with a one-week recovery.
If you twist and pain makes you fall, it's a Type 2 sprain with a one-month recovery.
If you twist and hear a pop, it's a Type 3 sprain with a one-year recovery.

All three sprains hurt and all three swell; the difference

is the healing time required. You can move on a sprained ankle the same day as the injury if you need to, but rest time is required in order to prevent it from happening again and becoming a permanently weak point in your structure.

The treatment of strains and sprains is the same regardless of severity. You won't likely have the main component: ice. Treat both with R.I.C.E. during the first 48 hours.

R: Rest, get off the injury and give it a break if you can. If not, favor it, a lot.

I: Ice reduces swelling during the initial 24 to 48 hours following a sprain or strain.

C: Compress the injured area using an ACE wrap elastic bandage for support.

E: Elevate the injury to take your weight off it and reduce the inflammation.

After the first 48 hours, the equation changes and you should apply heat to the damaged area, which increases circulation to the area and speeds circulation. So you keep the RCE and swap the "I for ice" with "H for heat" and get CHER. Remember: when you sprain you ankle, eat your RICE for 24 hours before meeting CHER.

Dislocation

Dislocation is a possible medical issue in the wild that is extremely painful but easily managed. It's also relatively easy to diagnose: when a shoulder is popped out of socket, for instance, usually from a bad fall, it looks grossly deformed and the person either cries to high heaven or passes out.

If someone else experiences this injury, follow these steps to relocate the limb:

Take a seat on the ground beside your patient.

Wrap something like a towel around his wrist so you can grip it; it will likely be sweaty.

Place your foot into your patient's armpit.

Slowly pull backward until the arm is stretched out towards you.

Let the arm slide back into place; the muscle will guide it there for you.

The arm will ache and not be right again for a long time but the immediate pain relief will be extreme and your patient will love you for it.

If you experience the injury, relocation is more challenging:

Wrap something like a rope around your wrist, padding it if you can.

Tie the other end of the rope to a tree.

Place your feet against the base of the tree.

Push yourself away at an angle so the rope extends your arm.

Allow your arm to pop back in.

Try not to pass out.

The same principles apply when a leg is dislocated to the front or back. Instead of placing the foot into the armpit, you'll use the groin, so mind your manners and pull like heck. Common sense will help you get the leg back into the groove; you'll know it when you've done it.

Fractures

Fracture is a fancy name for a broken bone. There are many different kinds but it comes down to two major ones for the survivor.

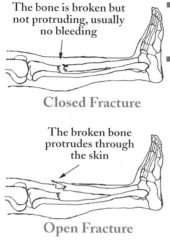

The bone is broken but not protruding, usually no bleeding

Closed Fracture

The broken bone protrudes through the skin

Open Fracture

- **Closed fractures** break the bone but keep everything still inside the person.

- **Open fractures** are the kind where the bone is not only broken, but it's decided to go and stick out of the person's body. These present the additional problem of deciding whether to try and put the bone back in or not.

The fracture checklist will move you through the few key considerations for treatment:

Assess bone

These indicate the presence of a fracture.

Check for an obvious deformity like a right angle where it shouldn't be.

Check for *crepitus*, a crunchy sound of moving broken bones around.

Be gentle and don't cause additional damage even though you must feel and manipulate a bit.

If there is pain upon any manipulation or movement of the joints, consider the bone broken.

Assess flesh

If the answer to any of these is "no," you've got repairs to do before splinting:

Pulsing: Is there a pulse below the fracture?

Temperature: Is the part of the fractured limb below the break as warm as the part above it?

Feeling: Does the patient have feeling in the part below the break?

Movement: Can they move anything below the break?

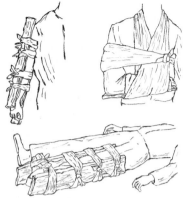

Splint Preparation

Preparing to splint a closed fracture

If there is no major deformity, you can splint the break mostly as it is. If there is some major bend in the road, you have to move it.

Normally, you'd only move it enough to get a general sense of normalcy and to keep the pulse flowing so the limb doesn't lose circulation and die, but, for the survivor, the chances are that you will be there awhile so you must consider moving a highly deformed broken bone so that it can heal properly. That means moving the deformity all the way back to a normal position. Follow these guidelines when doing so:

- Assess the patient's pulse before and after the manipulation. The pulse must be kept open.
- If the limb is cold, there isn't enough blood flow and

you'll need to move it some more.

- Stroke the patient's skin with your fingernail to assess whether he has feeling. If so, great. If not, that's not great but it's okay.
- The same goes for whether your patient has function or not. If he can wiggle his fingers or toes, super. If not, it can wait.
- If your patient can wiggle an extremity, see how much strength he has by having him push a little against your hand in all the normal directions.
- The key is to keep the same amount of function after splinting as your patient had before you applied the splint.

Assessment is important because it allows you to make sure you are setting their splint the best you can without the benefit of x-rays.

Preparing to splint an open fracture

You will encounter additional challenges from an open fracture. All modern medical practice says not to put the bone back inside. This is mostly correct except if you are in some jungle and think you're going to be there a while since an open bone is a lot like a highway for bacteria with a big neon sign sayin' "Come on in!"

If you have nice clean dressing to place on the bone, and can pad it so it doesn't get bumped or moved around, then this is the recommended course of action. Dress it and keep the dressing dry, not wet, so it doesn't invite more bacteria in. Pad and protect the break, splinting the limb the best you can, and keep the patient immobilized.

If you are sure help is nowhere near and dressings and antibiotics are in short supply or nonexistent, consider placing the bone back inside and letting the body be the dressing and the immune system be the antibiotics. Clean the bone the best you can before you place it back in the body. This is how it was in the days of old; they didn't leave the bone hanging out since there was no choice. The break might not have healed right, but it healed and the patient lived and so can you or your patient.

Splinting a fracture

The principles of splinting are simple:
Splint broken bones in a functional position or as close to it as you can get.
You can use boards or sticks or anything inflexible as a splint.
Tie the splinting board in two places above the fracture and two places below it.
Immobilize one joint above the fracture and one joint below it.
Pad all the boney parts to avoid causing ulcers or sores.
Reassess the pulse after you place each tie to avoid cutting off circulation.
Use ice and heat to promote healing as with sprains and strains.
If you have them, use anti-inflammatory drugs like aspirin or Motrin for fractures, strains and sprains. If the wound was open, use antibiotics if you have them.
If you have nothing, use an anatomical splint. Tie the broken limb to the body to immobilize it. Tie a broken leg to the other leg, tie a broken arm to the chest, etc. Broken fingers and toes are easily taped to the neighboring good digit.

Cricothyroidotomy

When there is simply no other way to get an airway open on someone because of trauma or anaphylaxis, consider making a hole in the neck. It's not as bad as it sounds.

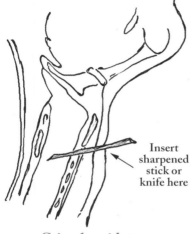

Cricothyroidotomy

Insert sharpened stick or knife here

Find the Adam's apple, which is the highest bump on someone's neck near the "voice box."

Just below that, you'll feel a dip and, below that, another less protruding bone. That dip is where you want to make a hole.

In a neat environment, you'd lift the skin there and make a one-inch incision across the throat so it leaves a less noticeable scar later.

In an emergency, stick your knife in sideways and poke through the skin and the cartilage.

Turn your knife so the blade opens the cartilage more and props it open so air can get in and out of the hole.

Stick something in there to hold it open—your finger if you have to—but do not let the hole close back up. (There will be only a little blood but enough to make it slippery.)

The hole can be closed up when the swelling goes down in your patient's mouth or when you clear the traumatized tissue out of the airway.

Amputation

Some principles guiding amputation:
Cut as low as you can and save as much as you can, especially the joint. I hate to say it, but for most people, cutting through the bone is too difficult, especially without anesthesia so cutting through the joint is exactly what you'll end up doing.
Wrap the limb tightly to squeeze as much blood out of that part as possible before you lop it off.
Apply a tourniquet about two inches above where you intend to slice.
Start slicing. Good luck!
Once the limb is severed, treat it like any wound. Stop the bleeding and apply a stump dressing. If the bleeding won't stop, consider cauterizing.

- **Cauterizing** should be considered if all other attempts to stop the bleeding fail or you are alone and can't tie off the bleeders yourself. Of course, you'll need a fire, so be sure to have this built before the chopping part starts. Use metal, like your knife blade. Get it red hot and touch it to the flesh and it will sear it and seal it shut.

- **Maggot therapy** is an all-natural alternative to manual debridement. Let some flies on that wound and cover it up. When the maggots show, let them eat until it hurts, then clean off.

Toxic critters

There are three main categories of toxins.

- **Hemotoxins** get into your blood stream and cause the

rupturing of cells. These symptoms usually present with blood at the bite site and pain.

- **Neurotoxins** paralyze the victim by attacking the nervous system and cause death through respiratory failure. The key indicators are very little pain and heart palpitations.
- **Cytotoxins** destroy cells. The concern for the survivor is the Brown Recluse spider.

Snake bites

The treatment for snake bites is simple. Keep calm.
Remove rings, watches or any articles of clothing near the bite that might cause constriction once the person swells up.

Do not:

Cut. This will only cause wounds while letting the venom contact more blood.

Suck with your mouth. The venom will get absorbed into your blood stream too!

Use ice. Not like you'll have any, but it won't help, though it won't really hurt either.

Use a tourniquet. The venom will get in anyway and this hurts the limb if there is no venom.

Do:

Use suction devices if within the first 3 minutes.

Use a constricting band two fingers wide and two fingers **above** the bite—**between** the bite and the heart. The difference between a constricting band and a tourniquet is that you should be able to get two fingers under a constricting band but not a tourniquet.

> **Treat the symptoms.** If you suspect a hemotoxin, try not to give aspirin as that is a blood thinner and will only speed up hemorrhaging.

> **Clean and dress the bite.** Always apply the principles of wound management.

The truth is that bees kill more people every year than snakes do.

Other biters

- **Scorpions, spiders, ants and wasps** bite too. They hurt but most either do not inject venom at all or rarely inject enough to be dangerous for healthy, full-grown adults. Children, elderly people and, unfortunately, weak and famished survivors can succumb to these venoms.

  For most bites of this nature, wilderness first aid treatment calls for *cryotherapy* or ice. Chances are, you won't have it so clean the wound, dress, it, keep your patient calm and look for signs of hemo- or neurotoxin. Remove stingers gently, by scraping away from the point of entry so as to not push more venom into the injection site. Gently brush off furry little, brightly colored critters like caterpillars as these things can sting and some have barbs.

- **Spiders** come in many shapes and sizes and a bite is a bite, but if you get bit and see the spider the basic rules of which ones have venom are these: **yellow, red or white spots** and **dark black or brown bodies.** Most spiders do not kill humans except for the Australian Funnel spider.

- **The Brown Recluse** is a little brown spider which often people don't know they've been bitten by, until they find a little swollen area with blister and a bulls-eye look. It might have a little pain that, after a few hours, turns itchy.

The reason is that this spider injects a cytotoxin that kills cells. What's happening is that ALL the tissue is being killed: the nerves, the blood, the muscle, everything is being destroyed. Usually, the toxin wears itself out as it spreads and stops killing cells. The skin usually stays on the top, looking dead and grey until the whole thing sloughs off and leaves a small crater.

Normally, the cytotoxin wears itself out after only one to two inches but wounds have been known to be up to 10 inches. This becomes significant when a person can't afford to lose six or seven inches of flesh at the bite location. As they're not aggressive, most Brown Recluse bites are on the butt or back from sleeping on these spiders. But if bit on the neck or face, you might not want to let the necrosis spread. A medical person would excise or cut it out to stop the necrosis. Treat what's left like all wounds.

- **Bees** deserve special mention because they kill. Avoid these.

Worms

As a survivor, there is a good chance you'll get them as you'll be subjected to uncontrolled food and water sources. Mostly, you'll be fine, and they'll have little impact immediately. But in some circumstances, they might immediately cause poor health. For these reasons, I address them in the chart below.

Worms and Treatments

Type or Name	Cause/ Transmission	Signs/ Symptoms	Treatment
Hook worm (Nematode)	Get into skin, usually when barefoot	Itching early, one week, maybe, but then not much until late when they might cause abdominal or respiratory problems	Albendazole, can use ice during first week to kill them while still migrating into deeper tissues
Roundworm or Strongyloidiasis (Nematode)	Penetrate skin from soil, migrate to lungs and intestines	Abdominal and respiratory problems	Thiabendazole
Tape or Flat worm (Cestode)	Undercooked or raw meat, burrow into muscle	Major stomach pain, flatulence, vomiting	Praziquantel
Pinworm, also called **threadworm** (Nematode)	Lives in the upper colon, sometimes gets into vagina, not found in tropics	Doesn't harm much but causes itching at night around the anus	Piperazine
Round Worm, Ascaris	Gets in through contaminated food	Usually no symptoms until late, when worms are found in stool, fever, abdominal pain	Mebendazole

Whip worm, Trichuriasis	Usually from soil ingested on food	Often no signs but can cause bloody diarrhea	Mebendazole
Cutaneous Larva Migrans CLM, also called **sandworm** (Nematode)	Gets into skin and lives just under the surface, usually on beaches, sand	Itches and leaves burrow trails, dies on its own in weeks to months	Albendazole, cryotherapy also called freezing with ice, using some cold aerosol spray might help
Dracunuliasis or Guinea Worm from Cyclops water flea	Drinking water with flea, worm gets into gut, migrates to lower legs, grows	Will take a while, maybe six to 12 months then forms a blister that itches a lot	Simple cloth filter on water will keep out water fleas, cut boil and slowly pull out worm

Rabies

Hard fact of life: rabies cannot be cured!

There are preventive vaccines that will help increase the chances of the post-exposure vaccines working. The post-exposure vaccines will work most of the time if given early enough. The incubation period is about two weeks to two months but can be as long as two years. Once rabies kicks in and the first signs appear, there is no hope of surviving, no matter what level of medical care is available. So, here's what it means to a survivor:

Treat all aggressive animals as if they have rabies. Avoid being bitten.

If attacked by an animal under circumstances that seem out of character, assume rabies exposure.

Make all attempts to get to medical care ASAP.

If you or another survivor starts to manifest rabies symptoms, consider quarantine measures for the protection of everyone else.

PRIMITIVE PLANT MEDICINE

How and when to ingest medicinal plants

There are simply way too many plants to know them all. Try to know a few from each category and/or each region of interest. Once you know a few, there are a good many ways to render them but it comes down to these main three for a survivor.

Teas: mix something with hot or cold water and drink the fluid

Concoctions: something chunky like a slurry soup

Paste: anything mashed up and mixed with little water, mostly for topical application

Always have positive identification before using any plant.

Antibiotics (counter-infectives, really)

Honey: Use it like a paste as a topical antibiotic on wounds. Drink it with teas, especially for sore throats.

Salt water: Gargle as a mouthwash to control cavities.

Also, use it as a wash for wounds.

Onion: A natural low dose antibiotic, you can eat it or crush it and put it on wounds.

Garlic: Same story. Make a paste and cover wounds with it.

Broadleaf leaves: Good as wound dressings for their antibiotic properties. Consider cabbage leaves, mullein leaves (don't eat seeds) and plantain leaves in particular.

Tobacco: Use as a paste for wound care to take advantage of its antibiotic properties.

Mullein tea: is a good anti-infective for throat and mouth.

Oatmeal: Apply topically to use antibiotic properties.

Vinegar: Works well for cleaning wounds.

Clover: Use as an eye wash for conjunctivitis or as a vaginal douche.

Dandelion root: Boil into a concoction for use on acne and eczema.

Oak bark: Boil into tannin that's good for unbroken skin rashes. Don't drink.

Fruit pomace: Citrus and other rinds have antibacterial properties.

Booze: Outside of iodine and rubbing alcohol, alcohol is good for wound cleaning and it tastes good too and might come in handy around amputation time.

Eyes, ears, nose and throat treatments

Sore throat: Treat by ingesting tea made with plants containing vitamin C such as pine needles, rose hips or any citrus plant.

Hemorrhoids: Use oak bark, willow bark, witch hazel bark and leaves as well as any tea or tobacco.

Congestion: Topically apply toothpaste under the nose. Also, pepper can help clear the sinuses.

Earaches: Onion juices can ease these; just squeeze, add some water and rinse.

Throat aches: If you can find it, cinnamon is very good for the throat.

Dental

Cavity pain can be eased by oil of clove, salt water or draining pus.

Fillings lost can be replaced with wax or twigs as a stopgap measure.

Broken teeth can be repaired with super glue.

Knocked-out teeth, if still whole, can simply be put back in!!!

Extraction can be done in a worst-case scenario. It's difficult but better than excruciating pain and uncontrolled infection.

Anti-diarrheal

Mint teas: Soothes mild tummy aches.

Sassafras: Calms abdominal cramps.

Hazel leaves: Relieves stomach upset.

Rose hips: Reduces discomfort.

Apple pomace

Oak bark: The tannic acids in this and many other hardwood trees' barks are helpful for mild diarrhea. To make tea, boil the bark for two hours; it will make a vile smelling and tasting concoction that will help. Repeat every two hours until stoppage is achieved.

For worst-case scenarios, **grind chalk, dried bones, and/or charcoal** from the ashes of your fire and make a slurry, suck it down and repeat every two hours until stoppage is achieved.

Antacids

Ash, charcoal, chalk and bones in a lighter brew than the anti-diarrheal slurry above will calm an acid tummy.
Dandelion, mint and sassafras leaf teas also help.

Anti-constipation

Soap will lube and stimulate a bowel movement.
Oil of any type that is ingestible will lube the guts.
Dandelion root concoction is good too.

Urinary problems

Yams help decrease urinary tract infections.
Dandelion tea eases discomfort.
Rose hips tea eases discomfort.

Antiseptic

Peat moss is an ancient treatment for wounds as it absorbs well and has a highly anaerobic acid, which inhibits bacteria from growing.
Urine is sterile and if it's all you got, whip it out.
Oak bark and many hardwood barks boil down for tannin juices.
Dock leaves

Anti-parasitic

A worm-removal stick can be used for Guinea worms. Cut the blister, pull a small piece of the worm out, wrap it around the stick and then slowly pull and spin, wrapping the worm like spaghetti on a fork.

Kerosene, taken once in a two-tablespoon dose, will clear out gut worms. Don't repeat for 48 hours.

Salt. Mix four tablespoons with one quart of water to do the same.

Cigarettes. Eating one-and-one-half cigarettes will shock gut worms enough to make them let go and pass.

Tannic acid. The inner bark of hardwood trees can have this effect.

Hot sauce and/or peppers as part of a regular diet can reduce parasite loads.

Fern stems. Crush the subterranean root into a powder that is known to fight parasites.

Jesuit or Mexican tea. Make a strong concoction that goes by this name from the seeds of a common weed in the South-Central desert region that smells like licorice, fennel or anise.

Insect repellents

Garlic or onion rubbed all over the exposed skin can also be consumed afterwards and sweated out pores.

Oak bark boiled into tannin is good as insect repellent. Don't drink it in this treatment.

Smoke from a fire or cigarette will help keep bugs away.

Sassafras leaves for bedding. The scent keeps 'em away.

Mud covering exposed skin makes it harder for insects to get a blood meal.

Make a face screen with cut-up strips of cloth.
Tobacco can be used as a skin rub and for smoking.
Pepper rubbed all over keeps bugs at bay.

Analgesics (Pain relievers)

Strangling fig root: Smoke the dried root.
Garlic juice: Paste for skin and joints.
Onion juice: Paste for stings.
Yams: Reduce muscle spasms and fever.
Clover: Good for bites and stings, also good as an eye wash for infected eyes.
Coca leaves: When chewed, these have a good analgesic effect!
Willow bark: Boil to make a tea or just chew the bark.
Toothpaste: Apply topically for heart burn.
Pepper: Reduces joint paint and muscle spasms.
Oatmeal: Has pain-relieving properties, also has antidepressants.
Coconut meat, ash, mud, dandelion paste: Relief from stings of bees, scorpions, spiders, centipedes.
Bleach: Remove poison ivy, oak and sumac. (Also, use ash or drying agent to absorb resin from these plants.) Bleach can also be used to treat chiggers (any smothering agent like sap will also work).

Anti-inflammatory

Willow bark: Tea for systemic inflammation, paste for topical application.
Aspen bark: Soak the bark and lay on the affected area.

Anti-hemorrhage

Puff ball mushroom: Helps the blood clot.
Plantain leaves: Can stop bleeding as a vasoconstrictor.

Anti-fungal

Onions: Rub on infected area.
Toothpaste: Has fungicidal properties, apply topically.

Anti-pyretic (Counters fever)

Willow bark tea
Aspen bark tea
Oak bark tea
Yams

References

The U.S. Army Special Forces Medical Handbook
The U.S. Special Operations Forces Medical Handbook
*The U.S. Joint Personal Recovery Agency Survivor's First
 Aid Course*
The Emergency War Surgery Book
The Merck Manual
The Wilderness First Aid Manual

10

NATURE

The First Rule of Nature is to know the "R.O.E."—or Rules Of Engagement.

Hawke's Dirty Half-Dozen R.O.E.

- **Rule # 1—Know Thyself** Know what your strengths and weaknesses are, know who you are, and know where you are when in a *survival* situation. And before you find yourself in such a place, study and practice the essence of survivalin' at home and in the field. Learn about your home surroundings, your neighborhood and outlying area, your routes to and from work, and also study any areas you may be traveling *before* you travel.

  It's only in the practice and application of yourself in test/practice/training scenarios, that you can really come to know yourself in the absence of the hardest and harshest test of reality. So, practice survival to understand your skills, abilities, and weaknesses *before* you have to put them to use.

- **Rule # 2—"Be Prepared"** It's the old boy scout cliché, but it's been around and stays around because it's true and it works. The better prepared you are now, the better you'll fare later. Can't say it any simpler, and no point in saying it any further.

- **Rule # 3—Forget What You Want** This is the big thing that crushes most people physically and spiritually. You might want to be home or anywhere other than where you are, but that clearly is not what happened. Forget about it for now. "What you want" won't help or change a thing. The only thing that matters is where you are, what you have, what you know, and what you can do.

- **Rule # 4—Do What You Must** This is really another way of saying "necessity is the mother of invention." Regardless of your feelings, opinions, biases, prejudices, perceptions, and religious or philosophical beliefs, anything that is not practical, pragmatic and that doesn't pass the common sense test, simply holds no sway in the survival situation. Do what you need to do to survive—eat strange foods, get naked to cool a fever, tear apart your clothes to make twine or bandages, spend hours looking for food and water, kill to eat, sleep with an enemy in the cold to stay warm, take the hand of an antagonist to be rescued—whatever it takes.

- **Rule # 5—Never Quit!** This should be said on every single page of this book, and in any book about survival. It is the essence of the entire field of study. Never quit!

- **Rule # 6—Forget the Rules** The one rule that applies to all rules is to know when to bend them and when to break them. But when it comes to survival, there are no rules, really. There are only guiding principles, founded on tried, tested and sometimes-true tenants. But the main thing is to not let the rules set any kind of limits or parameters on you that make you give in or succumb to some statistics spouted off by someone, somewhere, but not there with you. If the rules say you can't climb, but you need to, then by God climb!

Bug Out Bags, Aid Bags, and Survival Kits

In SF we operate on simple principles. Keep everything you absolutely need for survival on your person at all times. Everyone should have a knife, lighter, compass, and light on them every day, and everywhere they go.

Next, keep a mini-kit in your coat, or purse, or glove compartment, or desk. This has a little bit more like a condom and/or ziplock bag as a canteen, some foil for fires and signals and dressings, some longer-term fire-starters like a magnesium bar and magnifying glass, some vitamins, some meds, a sewing kit, etc. For us, these things were always on our vest or web-belt.

Then everyone in SF also had their actual "go-bag" — the butt-pack or extra magazine pouch or canteen pouch filled with some food, water, first aid, fire starters, signals, maps, compasses, bigger tools and/or weapons/knives, etc.

It is this three-tier system that I encourage everyone to have and live by. It's simple, it's easy, it works, and it's useful almost daily. So always keep: O.U.T.

On-You Kit—The minimal basics.

Urgent Kit—A bit too much to have on you at all times, but always ready to grab.

Travel Bag—The real deal you'll depend on for any duration of days.

See the charts on the following pages for items to include in your kits.

Hawke's Recommended Survival Kit Items

Backpack, medium size, easy and light

D-Ring for mounting to vehicle or aircraft or holding off–ground at camp site

Lighter, large and small (2)

Magnesium bar, fire starter

Matches, waterproof, waterproof container with whistle and compass

Whistle, with compass and magnifying glass

Compass, lensatic (military or civilian)

Water-purification tabs

Iodine drops (small bottle to purify water and treat wounds)

Electrical tape

Gauze, 1+ rolls for bandages, fire starter, toilet paper, etc.

Cravat—triangular bandage, tourniquet, sling, towel, sweat/drive-on rag, head protection, and as rag for filtering muddy water or gathering dew as well as additional pressure dressing

Soap, small bar, preventive hygiene/cleanliness

Toilet paper

Water (100 ml minimum)

Ziplock bag, large (canteen or food storage)

Trash bag, large (waterproof bag or rain coat)

Multivitamin pack

Meal bar

Beef jerky

Knife, small, Swiss style, with scissors, can opener, accessories

Knife, medium, Leatherman style with pliers, screwdriver, file, saw, etc.
Knife, large, fixed blade, utilitarian style, dual blade
Machete with saw on other side
Hammer/hatchet tool for chopping
Shovel tool (handheld or fold up)
Mag light, large
Mag light, mini
Batteries, spare, same for all items
Strobe light
Signal mirror
Pen flare, laser-type
Radio (shortwave) and transmitter
GPS & SPOT-type beacon transponder/locator
Space blankets (one as shelter from sun/rain, one as sleeping bag, two double as litter)
Net/hammock (back sack, bed, trapping, fishing, etc.)
100 feet of 550 paracord
10 safety pins
Fishing kit
Sewing kit
MRE or equivalent
Water, filter, canteen, and water containers
Canteen-style metal cup
Hunting rifle, ammo, and cleaning kit

Alternative hunting items like a slingshot, bb-gun, and bow and arrows
Now, apply these items to your car, boat, plane, home, office, and vacation home or survival shelter.
And multiply these factors by the number of family members, and increase times by the number of days you plan for. I start with 30 days, but 15 is more reasonable, and 7 is the minimum. Use 3 days at the very least

Never forget: "Every day above ground is a good day!"
And always remember: Never Quit!